Teaching to Learn

A Direction for Education

Guy Claxton

CASSELL

For Mary Anne

Cassell Educational Limited
Villiers House, 41/47 Strand, London WC2N 5JE, England

© Guy Claxton 1990

First published 1990

British Library Cataloguing in Publication Data
Claxton, Guy
   Teaching to learn: a direction for education.
   1. Learning by school students
   I. Title
   370.1523

ISBN 0–304–31904–X (hardback)
      0–304–31903–1 (paperback)

Typeset by Litho Link Limited, Welshpool, Powys
Printed and bound in Great Britain by
Biddles Ltd, Guildford and King's Lynn

Contents

Foreword

Guy Claxton is a troublesome sort of person. He isn't content to leave well alone. Not for him the standard theories and practices of education, the myths and beliefs, the folklore and the prejudices with which all too many educators are infected. In everything he writes, there is the explicit challenge to think again, to puzzle things out for ourselves, to go beyond the conventional and the comfortable, and to launch out on a voyage of discovery designed to bring us face-to-face with the realities of human behaviour. If he had lived in the Middle Ages he would doubtless have gone the way of all troublesome fellows and ended his days chained to a dungeon wall or, worse still, chained to a stake.

One reason why we should be grateful that we live in generally more enlightened times is that the Guy Claxtons of this world are allowed to go free and speak their mind. For in listening to them we are wiser men and women. In the present book Guy worries away at one of his favourite themes, namely how and why learning takes place. Dismissing the notion that we can have 'theories' of learning which explain the way we (and the children that as educators we teach in the school and in the home) acquire the skills and information and ideas that make us what we are, his starting point is that learning is essentially a *personal* affair. The way in which we learn (and the way in which we teach) is bound up with our unique personalities, philosophies and value systems. Thus to be a good teacher involves learning practicalities about ourselves, not just learning abstractions about the children we face each day in the classroom.

And indubitably he is right. One of the worst mistakes any teacher (or any adult who has to do with children) can make is to assume that learning failure is occasioned by something 'out there', in the child or children concerned, rather than by some breakdown in the complex interactive process involving teacher, child, and the material to be learned. A complex interactive process, moreover, which cannot but be specific to each learning experience and to the unique circumstances within which it is embedded.

There is of course a sense in which realizing this fact, and behaving accordingly, is a demanding business for the teacher. And in that sense this is a demanding book. It demands that the reader, whether experienced teacher, student teacher, politician or interested layman, look closely at his or her own assumptions about education, about children, about school learning and about oneself. Guy Claxton goes carefully and persuasively through models of the mind, through learning strategies, and through all the related issues of relevance to the educator. He argues his case with all the force that one would expect from a man with his long experience of commenting upon the learning process and of working with teachers. But he expects his readers to bring something of themselves to the book. He sets up a kind of dialogue with them, in which ideas are brought forward and bandied about until they collapse through their own lack of substance or take off on stimulating flights of the imagination. He encourages an activity of mind which leaves the reader feeling not only that he or she in a subtle way *owns* the book but (and this I know is what will please Guy Claxton most) wants to go out and make a much better job of helping children to learn.

In short, a book for all teachers and student teachers who want to be of greater service to children. And a book for all adults who care about education and who want to see it achieve its proper purpose of enhancing and enriching young minds.

David Fontana

Acknowledgements

Acknowledgement is gratefully made for permission to use the following material:

to Ronald C. James and the Weidenfeld and Nicolson Archives for the 'dalmatian' reproduced from R. L. Gregory, *The Intelligent Eye*, as Figure 4.2, page 75;

to Richard White and Basil Blackwell Ltd for the illusion reproduced from R. T. White, *Learning Science*, as Figure 4.3, page 76;

to the Open University for the figures reproduced from Guy Claxton's unit 'Classroom Learning' (Unit 13, Block 3 in Course E208, *Exploring Educational Issues*), reproduced here as Figures 3.2 and 6.1, pages 52 and 108, and for permission to quote some passages from that unit which formed the basis for some of the discussions in this book;

and to Daniel Dennett and Oxford University Press for the extract from D. Dennett, *Elbow Room*, reproduced on page 95.

Chapter 1

Why Education Needs Ideas

> I know of no safe depository of the ultimate power of the society but the people themselves, and if we think them not enlightened enough to exercise their control with a wholesome discretion, the remedy is not to take it from them, but to inform their discretion.
>
> Thomas Jefferson[1]

The most damaging consequence of the Education Reform Act would be if it were to persuade teachers, and others involved in the education business, that it was not worth continuing to think for themselves about education. Poor legislation can be changed, though it is a slow process. But it will only be changed if enough people have good ideas about how to improve it, and some sense of their ability to have an effect. If they feel powerless and clueless, prospects for change are diminished. If we are to work towards a form of schooling that is truly worthwhile for all young people – something that we have not yet devised, and which the present changes will not produce – the current reforms must signal to people the renewed necessity for educational debate, not its futility.

So if it is unfashionable to be thinking positively about the future rather than reactively about the present, and to be dealing with ideas and possibilities rather than pragmatics and expediencies, then this book is profoundly out of style on both counts. I take this to indicate that it is all the more timely, all the more necessary; not so much because I want to promote my ideas about 'good learning' as the only solutions to the problem of how to educate young people well, but because I believe it is vital that debate happens at the level of the big questions as well as at the level of Records of Achievement, Attainment Targets, special educational needs and conditions of service. One of the reasons why there is little concerted opposition to the current reforms is that there is a lack of intelligible ideas around in teachers', parents' and governors' culture with which to frame high-level critiques and alternatives. I want in this book to contribute to the discussion, and if possible to foment it.

A KIND OF PSYCHOLOGY

The language I speak is psychological, and I see such a language as having clear functions and limitations. It is not the business of psychology to indicate what education should be, nor what counts as the 'best' form of schooling: that is the province of aims and ideology. But it can help in the process of influencing people's actions, attitudes and aims by showing what the range of options are, and what conditions are needed to achieve each of these options if chosen. It can also show which goals are compatible, in the sense that they are targets which can be hit with the same educational shot; and which require different, even conflicting approaches.

This is a useful job because educational thinking at the moment tends to swing between grandiose rhetoric, which is quite out of touch with what schools, at least in their current form, are able to do, and piecemeal pragmatism, which is useful, but does not add up to any coherent view of education as a whole. The rhetoric confuses teachers and pupils, and is based on wishful thinking. The pragmatism often feels like too little, too late. The psychology I want to present steers between these alternatives by offering a grounded view of what young people are actually doing in schools, and of what it might be possible for them to achieve. I want it to be clear-sighted enough to tie people's sense of what is desirable to what is possible, but also to expand the range of possibilities, and to indicate what is required to make them real. Governors, teachers and parents might thereby be assisted to make more intelligent choices, and to mount more powerful campaigns.

To achieve such an aim, a book must be not only clearly

conceived but clearly and persuasively expressed. So although the focus is psychological, it is neither an exposition of research nor even-handed. I have drawn widely on areas of contemporary theory and data, but for the most part I have left these dissolved in the argument as it progresses and have not made them explicit in the text. And I have been unashamedly selective in the scholarly foundations I have chosen: my aim is to argue a case, not to provide an unbiased psychological review. I run the risk, therefore, of offending the academics, especially those whose stances and loyalties are different from mine. For them, and for others who would like to appraise for themselves the evidence on which my claims are based, I have provided notes at the end of each chapter which reveal the most important sources, and, where appropriate, some comments on the major alternative points of view and areas of current dispute.

WHO IS THE BOOK FOR?

I have three particular target audiences in mind for the book, and I would like to address a word to each of them. The first comprises those who have control, in some way, large or small, over educational policy. Specifically, in these days of increasing parent power, I want to address those who sit as school governors or on education committees, or who otherwise have an active voice in children's education. The risk entailed by this devolution of responsibility (if that indeed is what is happening), as the quotation at the start of the chapter says, is that 'the people' will make decisions that are well-intentioned, but which are born of a limited sense of what is possible, and of channels of educational thinking that will necessarily have been laid down by their own schooldays. John Watts, ex-principal of the pioneering Countesthorpe College in Leicestershire, puts the problem, perhaps a little harshly, like this:

> The educational system has always displayed great inertia, a built-in resistance to change, which is contributed to by both teachers and parents alike. Teachers, enjoying tenure, will resist any radical departure from the attitudes and practices they acquired in initial training and, more particularly, during probation: nobody wants their own established expertise threatened. Parents, on the other

hand, however much they have suffered at school, or even if they left it with a sense of failure, usually attribute the shortcomings to themselves rather than to the system, and thus find it difficult to envisage school in any form other than the one that they themselves experienced.[2]

If governors and others are to use their power wisely, it therefore behoves them to be as well advised as possible about the educational options that are available, and the requirements, consequences and pitfalls of each – and not just at the level of day-to-day management, but more broadly too. Moreover, if teachers are feeling held back by conservative (with a small 'c') bodies of parental opinion, then they must undertake the task of educating that opinion. I hope that this book will be written clearly enough to serve as helpful ammunition.

The second target audience is teachers who are already established members of the profession, and who are undertaking any form of in-service training, or who are reflecting privately on the value of what they are doing, the directions in which they might like to develop their careers and the freedom that they have to do so. My recent book *Being a Teacher: A Positive Approach to Change and Stress*[3] explores the difficulties of keeping up your interest in change and personal development at a time when it looks as if more and more responsibility is being taken away from you. But it has relatively little to say about the forms that such development might take. It focuses more on the process of change than on any particular aims (though the last chapter foreshadows the conclusions about teaching for learning that the present book aims to justify). Indeed, one of the things I want this sequel to do is to provide a psychological rationale for this shift in the direction of education, one which so many teachers would like to occur, towards the empowerment of young people to be enthusiastic and confident learners, and away from the concern with their acquisition of predetermined, scholastic skill and knowledge, and the accumulation, if they are lucky, of certificates.

Another way in which the book may help teachers undergoing change, whether voluntarily or reluctantly, is in highlighting the importance of people's belief systems. Once you have mastered the art of teaching, the social mores of your staffroom and the rudiments of the National Curriculum well enough for life in school to have become somewhat routine — though I am aware I might be writing for teachers two or three years down the line from 1990 — you may well start wondering what exactly it is that you are doing. Apart from French or chemistry or music, what is it that you are teaching or transmitting during your daily encounters? The answer, of course, is that you are teaching yourself – who you are, what you believe in, what you stand for, both as an individual and as an employee of the education system. Underneath the melody of the lesson content there are always the harmonies of your attitudes and beliefs. Beginning to take an interest in these is an uncomfortable process for which many people do not have the energy while they are still learning the job. In addition, the changes that are being instituted around you, and over which you have little or no control, may be increasing the urgency of the difficult question of whether you are being, and are allowed to be, the person that, in your better moments at least, you would lik to be. I hope that the book will provide some support for such an enquiry.

Finally there are student teachers, those doing B.Ed. or PGCE courses, or other forms of qualification which may be in being by the time this book is published. Your dominant concerns are practical, and you, like generations of students before you, will be rightly sceptical of any offerings that do not bear directly and obviously on the business of learning to teach. What I want to talk about will help in two ways. First, it will help you understand what is going on in the classroom, especially below the surface, so that your interactions with pupils are more timely and effective. Second, it will help you make sense of the experience that you are going through as you learn to teach. There are strong parallels between what is going on in the privacy of pupils' minds and the personal, even emotional, issues that are facing you. For both groups the unseen pressures of self-esteem and social standing influence markedly the direction that learning takes and the ease with which it proceeds. I shall try to point out these similarities as the study proceeds.[4]

What makes it possible to speak to three audiences simultaneously, and at the same time to tell a story about how young people learn, both in and out of school, is that there are common threads to the argument. I now want to outline what these are.

THE BASIS POINT OF VIEW

Learning always involves a modification of what you already believe or know. People's behaviour and opinions are the visible branches of an enormously complicated underground root-structure of ideas and assumptions, most of which we do not even know that we have. These 'implicit theories', as I shall call them, not only determine the way we behave: they also determine how we approach anything new – how we think about it, how we react to it, how we learn about it, even how we actually *see* it. Right from the very beginning, the moment we are born, all learning involves the proliferation and differentiation of what we knew the moment before. Thus the 5-year-old tries to make sense of his new teacher by first treating her like, and then gradually distinguishing her from, his own mother. The 14-year-old struggles with her physics in terms of intuitive analogies between electricity and water flowing down a pipe. The student teacher instinctively tries to teach in the way he himself was taught, and slowly learns that school contains many types of character different from those with which he is familiar from his own schooldays. The school governor, mother of the 5-year-old, feels intuitively that there is 'something wrong' with a primary school philosophy that no longer distinguishes between 'play' and 'proper learning', an attitude that she has unwittingly carried with her since her own early years.

What people are doing as they learn and change can be understood only in terms of the way their previous experience has set them to construe the new situation – and therefore learning can be guided and assisted successfully only in the light of this understanding. Most importantly, any suggestions that are offered to the learner must make sense in terms of the current approach she is using. They must be opportune, speaking to a felt need; intelligible, presented in the right terms; plausible, having face validity; and fruitful, seeming to provide useful implications and possible ways forward. If what is taught does *not* engage with current understanding in this way, it will be ignored, or, if it *must* be retained, certain rather special skills will have to be called upon. (People differ enormously in the extent to which they have developed these special skills, and it is this, rather than the level of some hypothetical 'ability', which accounts for much of the variance in school success.) It follows that when teachers really *know* that what learners are doing is editing, merging, splitting and relabelling what they already knew, they start to listen, to be sensitive to 'where the pupils are at', so that they can help them move on. They are less interested in simplistic diagnoses such as 'low ability' or 'unmotivated', and less likely to tease the 5-year-old for being babyish, scold the teenager for her stupid ideas, humiliate the student by pointing out all the things he did wrong in a lesson, or harangue the parent about her obstructive attitude and old-fashioned notions.

LEARNING IN SCHOOL

People's implicit theories about education in general, and learning in particular, determine what they see as being *wrong* with schools, and how to do it better. Everyone would agree, I think, that the point of school is for pupils to come to know, do or be more. We, and they, can consider their time in school well spent if, as a result of their attendance, they come to possess certain knowledge and understanding, certain skills and abilities, and certain personal qualities that we, and they, value. But within this general framework there is much room for disagreement about what abilities it is that pupils should have acquired. Some emphasize the mastering of bodies of knowledge, like who did what in medieval England or the kinetic theory of gases. Some stress the importance of skills like speaking French or the evaluation of evidence. And others consider that more personal qualities like confidence or a positive self-image are what is really important. Everyone who sees school as more than a social facility for allowing parents to go to work agrees that it is for some kind of learning.

But people are also concerned that learning in school is less successful, or more difficult, or more quickly forgotten, than it ought to be. Few teachers, parents or politicians are convinced that things are just right, and that school is working as well as it can or should. Few of the rest believe that the Education Reform Act is making a difference for the better that is anything like substantial enough. The explanations that they give provide the starting point from which to think about how to improve learning in schools, and the range of such diagnoses is as wide as the kinds of learning that people think education is for. Some say that the curriculum itself is boring and irrelevant (so we need a new curriculum). Some say that teachers are demoralized and that schools have a poor 'ethos' (so enthuse the staff and treat them better), or that there is lack of leadership (so send headteachers on management training courses), or diminishing resources (so 'fight the cuts'). Some say that the problem is the decline of moral standards or 'respect' in young people (so firmer discipline and clearer values at home and at school are required). Others blame the subject matter for being too difficult or not structured well enough, or the teacher for not explaining things clearly enough or for having expectations that are too low (so curriculum development or better teacher training are necessary). Still others say that learning is fine for some pupils, but not for others: the ones who are lazy or unmotivated (so get out the stick and/or carrot); those who have 'special educational needs' or 'learning difficulties' (requiring special attention to remedy them); or, worst of all, those who are 'low ability' (for whom there is, by definition, little hope).

All these diagnoses rest on particular views of learning: what it involves, how it works, and what impedes or facilitates it. For whatever one may say about the curriculum, or resources, or teaching methods, or discipline, it is in the mind of each individual pupil that the learning is or is not taking place. The learners' minds are the only point of contact between what the school is offering and what they will take away with them in the way of comprehension, capability or quality. So it is only by understanding accurately what is going on in learners' minds as they sit in classes (and chat in playgrounds) that we can see what effects these hypothesized causes and influences are really having. To help pupils learn, everyone concerned must be able to think in terms of the best learning theory available.

Thus I would argue that at the heart of education, and of our attempts to improve it, must lie an accurate understanding of the process of learning. If thinking is for the most part unwittingly channelled and limited by the implicit theories on which it is resting, then false or unfounded theories will inevitably send us looking for solutions to educational problems in the wrong places. Unfortunately the theories of learning that have been current in the educational world have usually been either those of unexamined common sense or obsolete models pilfered from experimental psychology. When people use the former they perpetuate the implicit explanations dissolved in everyday speech and prejudice, which are archaic and inaccurate. When they draw on the latter they are in danger of badly over-extending research that does not apply to the complex, shifting world of real children or adolescents in real classrooms. They try, as they have with Piaget, Bruner and other worthies, to force educational practice to fit a Procrustean bed of abstractions – ideas that somehow metamorphose into ideals – derived from studies of particular groups and ages that are surreptitiously transformed into universal, culture-free truths.

It is not only of genuine academic interest, therefore, but also of considerable practical importance to develop models of learning that steer their way between these two pitfalls of the woolly common sense and the quasi-scientific prescription. Much of current practice in schools, and the way people think about education, is still based on out-dated and inaccurate ideas about learning, whether derived from folk or formal sources. These ideas, buried in the minds of teachers, parents and administrators, limit what they can conceive of, and therefore constrain their sense of what is possible. Not knowing what is possible, the search for ways of doing what is desirable is improverished or even abandoned.

THE TRAILER

Let me now give a preview of the other main themes that the book is going to explicate, and to argue for. The first is the idea that our implicit theories do not constitute one vast, coherent body of knowledge, like the theory of relativity: rather they are a collection of lots of different, piecemeal, purpose-built 'minitheories' which we have accumulated for doing the range of jobs and solving the range of problems that we have encountered to date. Our factual knowledge and our 'know-how' are bundled up together in these packages, as instruction booklets, plans and sets of tools may be kept together on different benches in a workshop that are customarily used for particular kinds of job. Cognition consists of capsules of capability, each one dedicated to coping with events that arise within a familiar domain of experience. Thus functional distinctions between knowledge or 'content' on the one hand, and processes (or the tautologous 'process skills', a term which is fashionable in some quarters at the moment) on the other, are invalid. And this wreaks havoc with any attempt to teach general-purpose 'problem-solving skills'. Even the 'learning strategies', which I shall introduce in a moment, are not always readily available, but are tied to particular kinds of learning experience and appear only when their special 'prompt' is present.

We shall see, as the exploration of learning gets under way, that we are also forced to reappraise commonsense notions, based again on discredited psychology, of 'ability' and 'intelligence'. The mind does contain a natural learning ability which enables these minitheories to be tuned and developed in the light of experience. But this is only the beginning. As we grow up we are able to acquire extra abilities which come to function as 'learning amplifiers' or 'learning strategies'. With the aid of these we are able to accelerate our learning and to make it very much more safe and economical. So 'ability' or 'intelligence', far from being some innate, monolithic general-purpose quality given out in differing amounts, is in large measures an amalgam of these learning strategies.

This opens up another set of issues, for it must be the case that different learning strategies applied to the same situation will produce different kinds of learning product – an expanded capability, an insight, a recorded fact, a personal memory. Not all of these mental contents arise automatically; it is commonplace that each can occur without the others. So combinations of past and present experiences will lead to different events and repercussions in the learners' minds, depending on the learning 'set' that they happen to create, or that is already in place.

What you do as a teacher will influence (but it cannot determine) the way your pupils decide to learn in your lessons, and the sort of learning that therefore results. And the selection may be a good or a bad one. They may find out, in a tricky exam, for example, that they need some flexible skills when all they have are memorized facts. Or, to look beyond the classroom, people may find that, when trying to solve problems in relationships, they may have plenty of cleverness but not much insight. We shall see that this view of learning strategies has important implications for the conduct of schooling.

The next link in the chain is to ask where these strategies come from. The answer is that they are very definitely learnable – their repertoire is expandable – but equally definitely not trainable. The fact that they can be identified does not mean that they can be deliberately acquired through specialized practice. This is because an essential aspect of intelligence is knowing intuitively the power and limitations of each of the strategies – having a good feel for their appropriateness for different contexts and purposes – and *this sense can be developed only in situations where learners experience real choice and uncertainty*. Like all arts, learning relies on the subtle appreciation of events that arises gradually and spontaneously out of the prolonged exercise of responsibility – responsibility which may well be guided and constrained, but which cannot be reduced too far if the art is to develop.

This growth can therefore be supported but not engineered. It is possible to create environments in which this 'learning tool-kit' is reliably developed. However, contrary to wishful thinking, this goal of 'learning to learn' *cannot* be achieved with methods that are also trying to achieve some of the more conventional educational aims at the same time. This is an unpalatable psychological reality that it does no good to ignore, and that once faced, opens up the interesting question of at what ages different goals may be most appropriate, and/or how the separate strands can be interwoven. We will only be able to invent more powerful forms of schooling, I believe, when we have given up the naïve educational rhetoric which argues for a multiplicity of stools, only to persist in falling between them all.

The fact that learning is not of one but of many kinds opens up the question of how learners make the intuitive decision of how to learn. Clearly their choice is constrained by the nature of the learning experience and of the kind of 'steer' that is given to them, intentionally or unintentionally, by the way the learning environment is set up. But it will also be a reflection of their learning *habits*; of their current learning and other needs or interests at the moment; and also of the threats, real and apparent, that they perceive to be present. Thus the stance which young people adopt with respect to their learning reflects not only the opportunities to learn that are present, but the whole range of priorities that they bring with them. Attitudes to friendship, to success and failure, to authority as well as to themselves, all have an influence on the tacit decisions that are made about learning.

If this general analysis of learning is to be valid, it must illuminate the stances that young people adopt within the context of schools as they are at the moment, as well as showing the different attitudes that might be elicited by other contexts, both existing and hypothetical. For example, one particular inference is that, to learn in a way that is both judicious and courageous, a person has to assess the pros and cons of learning (and *not* learning) accurately. But the acquisition of an identity that is overly sensitive to failure and criticism stops the right decisions being made about what, when, where, why and how to learn. I shall argue that the ethos of school, again despite the rhetoric and even the widespread good intentions, works to produce such an identity in many pupils; and that, when this has happened, it becomes a matter of good sense for them to subordinate their wish to learn, and to learn *how* to learn, to the need to manage an increasingly stressful social situation.

LEARNING TO TEACH: A CASE STUDY

Before entering into the details of the new psychology of learning, I want to introduce it by illustrating some of its main features: particularly the importance of learning strategies, and the choice that people have, depending on the strategies they possess, to learn in different ways; and the impact on the learning process of the learners' pre-existing implicit theories. I shall use the example of learning to teach. If you are a student teacher, I hope the discussion will sound familiar. If you are not, I hope you will be able to focus on the more general points that I am trying to illustrate.

The first thing that strikes many such students is that learning to teach is surprisingly different from most other kinds of formal learning. The place of intellectual knowledge, understanding and skill, for example, is very different from that in an A-level or an undergraduate course. There the declared outcome is to pass an exam, and what is required to do so is to remember things (facts, theories, formulae, explanations); to have intergrated them, as far as possible, into some coherent understanding that enables you to manipulate what you know (create arguments, discuss issues, solve problems); and to have acquired a range of basic skills that allow you to accumulate information (reading, taking notes, doing experiments, using libraries) and to express it (writing, contributing to discussions, drawing graphs, deriving equations).

Now to become a teacher a certain level of proficiency in these general areas is presupposed. They are required in order to take part in a teacher training course, and they are necessary tools too for the practising schoolteacher who has meetings to take part in, report forms to fill out and new curriculum materials to appraise. But during teacher training they are instrumental, not focal. They are not an end in themselves (as they are at school and university) but a contributory means to the greater end of acquiring the art of teaching. And beyond a certain level of resourcefulness, critical ability and fluency, it does not seem to matter how 'clever' you are – because other kinds of learning, and other personal qualities, are just as important, if not more so. In particular, learning to teach is a more practical, more personal and often more emotional business than people are used to as undergraduates. So people who come into a teacher training course with strong implicit theories of what learning in an institution is like, derived from their previous education, can be in for a nasty shock when they find out how different it is.

For example, most students' top priority (and anxiety) is 'Can I teach? Can I keep order? Can I get on with kids? Can I get my stuff across to them?' Their goal is definitely practical. What they want is competence. Often the implicit expectation is that this can be acquired through thinking and understanding – that people can learn how to teach by being told. But their experience sooner or later reveals the uncomfortable fact that understanding does not produce competence: it can contribute to it, and guide its growth, but it cannot bring it about. What is learnt in the verbal part of a 'minitheory' – in this case the developing minitheory called 'How to teach' – does not necessarily affect what is going on in the practical part. Instruction and understanding dissolve into skill only very slowly, as any sports coach will tell you. This is why, quite rightly, many students feel that the 'real' learning gets done on teaching practice. Practical exercises in planning lessons during college 'methods' courses are seen as helpful rehearsals. But the traditional 'educational studies' part of the course (now usually disguised with some more relevant-sounding name like 'Problems, topics and issues in education'), where students are invited to 'think about education', can be a big disappointment if both tutors and students are not clear about the limited role that intellect can play in the process.

In fact most tutors are coming to realize that there is all the difference in the world between being a pundit and being a practitioner, and many have moved towards a more problem-centred and student-centred form of learning, in which students' insight into their own implicit theories about education is seen as more valuable than externally derived scholarly knowledge. But if their attempts to promote this amount to little more than watered-down academic seminars of the 'Now then . . . what do *you* all think?' variety, they are likely to fall just as flat. Students conditioned by their undergraduate studies to see seminars as vigorous, content-oriented forums for academic debate are bound to see such sessions as 'waffle', rather than as an effort to promote a different *kind* of learning.

This example highlights an important general aspect of the responsibility of the teacher or tutor: to set the learning situation up in such a way that learners' approaches to the learning task are channelled into appropriate directions – ones that will deliver the kind of learning that is actually going to be useful – and away from blind alleys. As we have seen, students may arrive from previous courses of study with firmly embedded implicit theories of what 'real learning' is like: analogies in terms of which a teacher training course will look 'soft' or 'ill-defined'. So part of the tutors' role must be to ensure that such unhelpful analogies are made explicit and that people are enabled to see how *this* experience is different in intention as well as in form.

But the other part is to ensure that the running of the course – the way it is organized and assessed, the way students are treated and so on – is also appropriate to the desired kind of learning. The trap here, which generates the confusion and bad feeling that we noted earlier, is that the theories that the tutors espouse may be at odds with the ones they actually practise. The classic 'mixed message' is to encourage students into a reflective, personal way of learning – and then hit them with a three-hour unseen written examination. Recent research has shown that the more 'academic' the content, the more formal the learning situation and the more traditional the examination, the more likely students are to adopt learning strategies that deliver rote learning, or a shallow understanding, rather than practical competence.[5] But the same research has also shown that some students arrive with a fixed model of learning which they are remarkably resistant to giving up.

Despite all the pressures and expectations from outside, learners are always left with some freedom to choose how they are going to learn. For example, imagine a pupil in a lesson or a student (yourself perhaps) in a lecture listening to someone explaining something. There are a range of different activities that may be going on in your head, each of which will lead to a different learning outcome. You might be trying to remember as much of what the teacher is saying as possible, and scribbling as fast as you can without really thinking about what she is saying. This attitude produces, at the time, a kind of language-based learning that is fairly 'rote'. Little prior knowledge is brought to bear, and consequently the message is retained, if at all, in a surface form. Of course you may always do further work on this raw information at a later date, in order to turn it into something more meaningful.

But you might be trying to do that as you listen, so that your intellectual knowledge of the topic is being deepened and extended 'on line'. This involves mobilizing an existing minitheory that is reasonably coherent, though unfinished like a part-completed jigsaw puzzle, which you can use to interpret what you are hearing, these interpretations in turn forming sensible additions to the emerging picture.

Alternatively, you might not be interested in getting a deep understanding, or even (at that instant) in grasping enough to pass an exam, but are tuned in just enough to catch any interesting or self-evident or particularly memorable fragments that come along. In this case you are currently relying on your store of general 'social knowledge' which is set to pick up brightly coloured bits and pieces without looking for overall coherence. You are just as likely to be wondering about the stain on the lecturer's jacket, thinking about what you are going to do in the evening, or watching the building work going on over the road, as you are, at any moment, to be attending to the content of what is being taught. Teachers are often reminded how many of their audiences are in this mode when they read exam papers that keep referring to a vivid, throwaway analogy that they happened to use, while conspicuously missing the main point they were trying to communicate.

If the content permits it, you might be oriented towards picking up practical information, working knowledge that enables you to get things done rather than just to understand them. Your attention is set to detect instructions in preference to explanations, and you may therefore be impatient with an 'academic' or unrealistic presentation that does not deal with practicalities. You are aiming to improve your skill or performance at some practical task, and are looking for hints and tips that will act as guides for your first-hand explorations.

Again if the content and presentation permit it, there is also the option of seeking *personal meaning*, or insight, in what is being said. Here your concern is with your own implicit theories, and the way in which the lecture is putting into words aspects of your own experience that had previously been unconscious or unarticulated. If this is successful, you are responding to what is being said not in terms of its coherence, casual interest or practical value, but as if it 'rang true'. At its best such teaching feels as if it is helping you to identify, and to give voice to, things that were latent in your understanding — especially of yourself — but which had never quite risen to the surface before. You may look as if you are miles away, but inside all kinds of connections are being made.

Finally, there are all the options within which the subject matter of the lesson has no place at all. You have quietly (or not so quietly) declined the invitation to engage with what you are being officially offered, and are instead having a whispered conversation with the person next to you, doing the crossword puzzle under the desk or having a nice doze.

So if learning to teach is not primarily an intellectual process, it is not a purely technical one either. A teacher, like an engineer, an architect or a surgeon, has to acquire a complicated array of skills and a subtle appreciation of when and how to apply them. This takes a lot of fallible practice under the guidance of an experienced coach. But the abilities of the teacher are much more *personal* than those of the engineer; and the learning that goes into them is of a different order and, potentially at least, more threatening. Teaching is in part about putting together clear, interesting, well-judged lessons, but above all it is about relationships. (One of the shifts in attitude that tends to occur during teacher training course is from 'I teach maths' to 'I teach people'.) Unless one has a productive working relationship with a class, be they 5 or 16 years old, the best planned lessons or activities are going to achieve little.

So the ability to relate to large groups of young people of widely different temperaments, interests, ages and backgrounds (both individually and collectively) is paramount. This means being resourceful, flexible and tenacious. It means being willing to experiment with each new group until a way of working with it emerges. In today's schools, especially secondary schools, this working relationship may turn out to have a very different quality with different groups. It means having the willingness to keep trying – especially with difficult individuals – and to bounce back from the inevitable run-ins and setbacks. It means very importantly being able to keep, or at least to recover, your sense of humour and of perspective.

Additionally, the sense of quality of relationships with colleagues is known to be crucial in determining how much teachers suffer from stress. More generally still, in a profession that is characterized increasingly by conflicting demands and self-questioning, the personal resources to cope with uncertainty are becoming indispensable. In a time of considerable change, teachers themselves need to be good learners, and a central quality of the good learner is to know when to surrender to the need to explore and experiment, and when to hang on to the old methods and routines. In learning to teach, what makes you defensive and how you respond to feeling threatened (or nervous or ashamed or upset or irritated) are very much part of the process. And this involves learning about feelings and gaining insight into your own habits and reactions.

Learning to teach is a personal affair for another reason. The process of the course may challenge students' implicit models of higher education, but the course as a whole is bound to impinge on their implicit theories far more broadly. Whether you like it or not, how you teach and how you learn to teach are bound up with your own personality, philosophy and values. Somewhere inside there is a set of personal standards – whether tacit or articulated, ill-formed or carefully thought out – that determine what shocks you, interests you or angers you about schools, and that serve as the benchmarks which you will use to guide and evaluate your progress as a teacher.

As I indicated at the beginning of this chapter, in order to develop a teaching style, or to change one already established, people will therefore need to become aware of their prior assumptions and to modify them so that they become congruent with, and support, the new style. For if a way of teaching is merely grafted on from the outside and does not take root in a teacher's system of values and beliefs, it is unlikely to be adopted wholeheartedly, and it will be ineffective or lead to a sense of inner dissonance and inauthenticity. Part of learning to be a teacher, therefore, is the process of uncovering your own implicit theories and beliefs about children, discipline, what is 'worthwhile' and, as we have seen, learning itself; and assessing whether they truly represent and are compatible with the kind of teacher you want and need to become. You may discover that the implicit theories that have been absorbed without critical reflection from parents, teachers or the general ethos of your own schooling may not meet the needs of a new situation – a different kind of school, with different kinds of young people from those with whom you grew up. It may also turn out that these old habits of thought, when they are unearthed, are incompatible with other values that you have developed for yourself in the meantime.

You may, for example, have spent your schooldays with friends who were mostly of the same colour, sex, academic inclinations and interests as yourself, and with teachers who seemed to see their job (how could they have seemed otherwise?) as teaching a world full of young people who were pretty much like you. Out of such limited experience a tacit model of teaching and learning has been distilled that may be quite inadequate to cope with the realities of a teaching practice school. If your schooling took place in a rather traditional country grammar school, you will not have much of a feel for the varied and unprecedented demands of a multiethnic, inner-city school. Alternatively, if you grew up as a first-generation Asian girl in a tough comprehensive, you may not be prepared for the conservatism, intolerance and academic singlemindedness of adolescent boys in the top stream of the single-sex grammar school that still exists down the road.

Becoming aware of the assumptions that one has unwittingly

made, especially those based on hearsay and prejudice, about young people from other cultures, or who talk with 'posh' or 'common' accents, is an uncomfortable but a very important part of the process of learning to be a teacher. One's own implicit theories give one ways of interpreting other people's behaviour that may work well for strangers of one's own class, sex and culture, but which give less trustworthy readings when applied to different kinds of people. Think for instance of the misunderstandings that can arise from the avoidance of eye-contact by pupils from different cultures. Part of the student teacher's job is to become aware of such assumptions so that they can be put to the test of first-hand experience and therefore come to be supplanted by other, hopefully more accurate theories.

I hope that this rather general discussion of the process of learning to teach will have given the flavour of the approach as a whole. If I have managed to communicate the idea that intellectual learning is only one of the several kinds; that people use different strategies to learn in different ways; that the tacit decision about how to go about learning is based on implicit theories and beliefs, as well as on the 'objective' nature of the learning situation; and that people's beliefs about themselves constitute a particularly influential subset of these implicit theories – then I shall have achieved enough for the moment. In the next chapter I shall have to become a little more technical as we begin to explore in greater detail the nature of people's implicit theories about learning, memory and the way the mind works.

SUMMARY AND READING

The main lines of argument in the book lead to the following conclusions. First, the way people intuitively view learning determines the way they think about schooling. Second, learning is a matter of skill. Third, different learning strategies produce different learning outcomes, which are differentially suited to different types of performance and problem-solving in the world. Fourth, learning is educable. Fifth, some environments and forms of 'teaching' promote the enhancement of learning ability; others inhibit it. Sixth, school as it mostly exists does not value, in the way it works, the development of 'intelligence' in this sense.

Despite the rhetoric, its actual goals largely preclude this development. Seventh, it would be possible for schools to achieve this alternative aim if they chose, but they would look very different from the way they do now. And eighth, there is no *moral* reason why schools should seek to foster the development of young people's learning ability rather than, say, their ability to look cool and/or pass exams; there are, however, urgent practical reasons for doing so.

The position I am espousing here is called 'constructivist', and it can trace its intellectual roots back to the 'idealist' philosophy of Bishop Berkeley in the eighteenth century and beyond. In contemporary psychology George Kelly's book *The Psychology of Personal Constructs* is often credited with its revival. A good, succinct introduction, from a philosophical point of view, is provided by Paul Churchland's *Matter and Consciousness* (second edition). The strongest statements of 'radical constructivism' are to be found in a volume edited by Paul Watzlawick, *The Invented Reality*. Some similarities with my position will be found in Phillida Salmon's recent *Psychology for Teachers*, which is much more interesting than its title suggests. Constructivism arose as a cognitive opponent of the powerful school of 'behaviourism', which sought general laws of behaviour in the study of simple situations, and which disparaged talk of hypothetical mental entities and processes. Though there are very few behaviourists in this strong sense left, the arguments about inventing mental processes continue, their main proponents being students of the work of James J. Gibson.[6]

NOTES

(1)   Quoted by Lange, D. (1988) *Tomorrow's Schools*. Wellington: New Zealand Department of Education.
(2)   Watts, J. (1984) The changing role of the classroom teacher. In Harber, C., Meighan, R. and Roberts, B. (eds), *Alternative Educational Futures*. London: Holt Education.
(3)   Claxton, G. L. (1989) *Being a Teacher: A Positive Approach to Change and Stress*. London: Cassell.
(4)   This theme continues the line of thought of Claxton, G. L. (1978) *The Little Ed Book*. London: Routledge & Kegan Paul.
(5)   Marton, F., Hounsell, D. and Entwistle, N. J. (1984) *The Experience of Learning*. Edinburgh: Scottish Academic Press.

(6) Kelly, G. A. (1955) *The Psychology of Personal Constructs*. New York: Norton. Churchland, P. (1988) *Matter and Consciousness*, 2nd edn. Cambridge, MA: MIT Press. Watzlawick, P. (ed.) (1984) *The Invented Reality*. New York: W. W. Norton. Salmon, P. (1988) *Psychology for Teachers*. London: Hutchinson. A good recent discussion of Gibson may be found in Bruce, V. and Green, P. R. (1985) *Visual Perception: Physiology, Psychology and Ecology*. London: Lawrence Erlbaum.

Chapter 2

Implicit Theories

Who is there . . . that hath not opinions implanted in him by education . . . which must not be questioned, but are here looked on with reverence as the standards of right and wrong, truth and falsehood; where perhaps these so sacred opinions were but the oracle of the nursery, or the traditional grave talk of those who pretend to inform our childhood, who received them from hand to hand without ever examining them?

John Locke[1]

To see the value of the approach to learning that I am going to describe, it is necessary to see what it is an improvement on. Why do we need to talk of 'implicit theories', 'learning amplifiers' and the like? What is wrong with common sense? Surely it would not be *common* sense if there were not a lot of truth in it? And why do we need a new kind of psychological model? There seem, if anything, to be too many already. As I said in Chapter 1, the first job of anyone who is selling an apparent solution is to show the clientele that there is a problem, and that currently available products are not good enough. That is what I want to do in the next two chapters. First I am going to describe some aspects of people's implicit theories about learning and ability, and show how they often interfere with learning; and then in Chapter 3 I shall take a quick run through the kinds of model of learning that psychologists have to offer to education, showing how and why they have developed to the current point.

WHY 'IMPLICIT'?

Most of what we know we are not able to describe. We are aware of thoughts, perceptions, feelings, actions and so on, but we are not aware of where they come from. We have to accept the unconscious as a fact, not in the classical Freudian sense of the dark cellar where we try to hide away our most awful secrets and memories, but simply as the inscrutable source of most of our experiences and responses. We cannot say how it is that we walk, nor, as a rule, where it was that we learnt to talk with the accent that we do. We can have a feeling that someone close to us is upset without being able to say *how* we know. We find ourselves, on the first day in the classroom as a new student teacher, suddenly behaving in a strange way, and realise that somewhere below the surface we must have been harbouring a model of a teacher from our own schooldays. Someone throws us a ball and we reach out to catch it, without any consciousness of the complex calculations that must have gone into the prediction of its speed and trajectory. As we pass a bunch of girls in the corridor they start to giggle, and without a pause we feel hurt, certain without any question that we must be the object of their sniggers.

All our spontaneous reactions arise as a result of our interpretations of events; and these interpretations are the products of our own learning. Out of years of experience we have distilled habits, expectations, hunches and beliefs that are the basis for our current view of the world. Parts of this huge storehouse of learning are available to our conscious scrutiny: we know what it is we believe and why. But much, probably the vast majority, of it is known to us only through its effects, and is not accessible to introspection. It is like a computer program which controls the way that the computer operates but is not itself on the screen, open to inspection. We call these contents of mind 'theories' because, like scientific theories, they are generalizations drawn from experience about the way the world works, which are used as a basis for predicting and interacting with it. And many are called 'implicit' because, unlike scientific theories, we are unable to articulate what they are. Learning at its most general is the business of improving our theories, elaborating and tuning them so that they keep track of the changes in the world and come to serve us ever more successfully.

GENERAL FEATURES OF IMPLICIT THEORIES

These theories, which give rise to our 'common sense', have a number of general characteristics – apart from their frequent tacitness.[2] They are in some ways similar to scientific theories – though there are important differences. Our personal theories are not necessarily logical – much of what we 'know' is useful despite the fact that it would not bear much rational scrutiny. And they are often not general, far-reaching and coherent, like those of the scientist, but are rather piecemeal and purpose-built. In many areas of life, coherence is of much less importance than having a quick, efficient, situation-specific routine that you can run off without much thought. (It is unwittingly following such routines that leads us to catch the train we usually get, on the odd occasion when we actually want one going in the opposite direction.)

They are powerful determinants not only of what we think, but also of our spontaneous behaviour. They seem to be relatively stable: often they are remarkably resistant to change, even in the face of good evidence. People are quite able to declare, 'I don't care *what* you say. I still believe that . . .' (That is an issue for student teachers, who may come out of their training courses still convinced of the rightness of their original opinions, despite hours of discussions that showed – to others – how off-beam or simplistic those opinions are; and also for classroom teaching, where pupils' implicit theories are often equally resistant to change.) Yet it is true as well that people sometimes *do* change their minds when the conditions are right. Quite what this means we have already touched on: there has to be some sense of personal dissatisfaction with their way of looking at things, coupled with the availability of an alternative that seems intelligible, plausible and fruitful.[3]

Another feature of these implicit theories is that they often have greater control over some aspects of our behaviour than others. For example, it is not unusual for people to show a dissonance between what they say about an issue and the way they actually deal with it. We may profess a love for the classics, but spend most of our time reading thrillers. Teachers may concur with a pupil-centred view of teaching, but in the heat of the moment, in the classroom, behave quite differently. Adolescents may subscribe to one theory about AIDS in personal and social education (PSE) lessons, and quite another on the river bank in the dark. When a personal theory has control over what we say rather than what we do, it is sometimes called an 'espoused theory'; when it has more influence over how we actually behave, it is called a 'theory-in-action'.[4] The difference between opinion polls and election results shows the disparity very clearly.

The next point I want to make generally about these implicit theories, before we have a look at some of their contents, is their tendency towards simplification, overgeneralization and dogmatism. They have been picked up, for the most part, unconsciously and uncritically: the opinions or habits they contain seem to us to be 'common sense' precisely because we have never thought to question them. They appear 'obvious' or 'inevitable' or 'natural' ways to think or behave. When people from different cultures meet, for example, there is much room for misunderstanding as they act according to different acquired sets of 'manners' that seem, to each, the only right and proper way to behave. This causes trouble in multiethnic schools, where behaviour which to one group of pupils is deferential (such as avoiding eye-contact with an adult in authority) is to the adults involved a sign of insolence; or where an activity that the school requires, such as changing clothes for PE, is felt by girls from a particular culture to be 'unseemly' and an invasion of privacy.

Such theories are resistant to scrutiny, and are often held with a great deal of emotional force – witness (at the time of writing) the outcry from the Moslem world about the book *The Satanic Verses*. Supposed alternatives may be attacked – as in this case – or equally strenuously ignored. They may make no allowances for differences of opinion, or for the fact that 'circumstances alter cases'. At the beginning of a teacher training course, students' opinions about education sometimes reveal this black-and-white character. Statements are delivered that seem to be written on tablets of stone, and which are couched in terms of all, none, always and never. As the foundations of such attitudes are slowly uncovered by experience and discussion, and as they are put to the test, so they may not only change in nature but become more contingent, more differentiated, as well. People become more inclined to say 'It depends'. Adolescents are notorious for jumping from one dogmatic, absolutely obvious and incontrovertible opinion to another, depending on the people they happen to be with, or the mood they happen to be in, as they search for the security of some simple philosophy to hang on to in the midst of the vast swirling uncertainties in sexual feeling and personal style.

The next, crucial, point to make about implicit theories is that they frequently make no distinction between what is true and what is believed: if something is believed to be so, then to all intents and purposes it *is* so. Some of our beliefs are held provisionally: we know them to be conjectures, and are willing to revise them if things turn out differently to how we had supposed. But many of the beliefs that we have picked up and incorporated into our ways of looking at things are treated as reality rather than hypothesis. About such matters we do not believe we are right – we *are* right. As the anger rushes up, we are not conscious of *assuming* that this child is being insolent: we *know* she is, and we have no doubt that the anger is righteous. When someone in the staffroom is preoccupied and fails to say 'Good morning', how we respond, and feel, depends on which of our implicit theories happens to be nearest the surface. On one day we may think, 'Jane looks pretty harassed. I'd better wait until later'; on another, 'What's got into Lady Muck this morning?'; on a third, 'Oh help, I must have done something wrong. I wonder what I can have done to upset her?' Mostly we are not able to see these *as* interpretations, but view them as realities to be dealt with – by backing off, bridling or placating respectively (all of which may be no help at all to Jane, who has just received a letter to say that her father has had to go into hospital).

THE ORIGINS OF IMPLICIT THEORIES

There is a final distinction between everyday, implicit theories and those of 'proper' scientists, and this refers to their origins. Formal theories are often derived intellectually from the joint consideration of experimental results and earlier theories, whereas implicit theories are picked up to a large extent from three sources. One is our own first-hand experience of the physical world, out of which we construct our webs of expectations and predispositions. When crossing the road, for example, most adults are able to judge the speeds of passing cars quite precisely, so that they are able to launch themselves safely into gaps in the traffic. We learn about heat and gravity and animal behaviour from fires and falling over and playing with the cat. I shall refer to theories which were principally learnt in this way as 'gut theories'.

The second source is the everyday social world: the way the people around us talk and behave. Their speech and reactions reflect their implicit values and beliefs, and, through our daily interactions with them, as we learn to rub along, so some of their way of looking at things rubs off. Theories that derive principally from these informal social sources I shall call 'lay theories'. It should not be too surprising, for example, that having spent 15,000 hours or so ourselves as pupils in school, our implicit theories about education in general, and learning in particular, are heavily influenced by the models and ethos to which we were exposed. It is common knowledge in the teacher training business that the way students start to teach usually reflects quite strongly the way they were taught. It is also common for students to discover on teaching practice that these habits of thought and action are quite persistent, and may spontaneously subvert beliefs and intentions that are more consciously held.

Both the first two sources are informal. Our third source is much closer to the world of the scientist, for it consists of what we are explicitly told. Even before we learn to speak, we are being instructed by parents about how to behave and what is so, and this process is amplified at school, where the process of deliberate instruction is intensified. If this source comprises the explicit curriculum of education, the values and attitudes picked up from the second source constitute the 'hidden curriculum'. I shall call these 'formal theories'.

IMPLICIT THEORIES ABOUT LEARNING

Let us now illustrate some of the beliefs that have been found to underlie people's ways of thinking and acting in educational contexts. Amongst all the implicit theories that form the basis of educational practice, none is more significant than those that concern learning itself. The traditional model of secondary school learning was developed in the British public schools and was filtered via the grammar schools into the state system at large, where it remains embedded (and reaffirmed by the current reforms) in much school organization and many teachers' minds today. The dominant approach to primary education, on the other hand, derives more from the powerful influence of pioneers such as Montessori, and theorists of child development such as Piaget.

Recent research has shown that, while changes are being introduced to these underpinnings, and while also some more experienced teachers begin to question them, nevertheless the following key beliefs continue to provide much of the guiding framework for school ethos and individual teacher pedagogy.[5] It might be useful for you to use them as a self-assessment inventory, to help you reflect on the beliefs that your experience has led you to espouse. I shall present them at this stage without critical comment – though you will rapidly see that many of them are at odds with the picture of learning that I outlined in Chapter 1.

'Knowledge is objective. It is discovered by experts (mostly from universities) and, if it has made its way through the syllabus and textbook barriers, then it is *ipso facto* accurate and important. It is like diamonds that are mined (by a process called "research"), polished and then put on display for ordinary people to gawp at and make notes about.' This attitude is more common among science teachers, though it is found elsewhere too. (Note that we must keep in mind the distinction between 'espoused theories' and 'theories-in-action'. Many science teachers would now *espouse* an approach to science as a human creation, a network of conjectures, rather than as a body of immutable 'facts' hewn from nature by the painstaking application of a systematic method – yet in their daily lives as teachers they may give no sense that this is so, apart, perhaps, from the occasional informal discussion with the sixth form.[6])

Alternatively, science teachers may see their knowledge principally as *skill*, as comprising a set of useful abilities that range from the rather specific, like doing a clean titration, to the rather general, like 'making observations and deductions'. Maths teachers are sometimes undecided as to whether their subject consists of 'discoveries' or 'creations'; but mostly, like some of their science colleagues, and many language teachers, they are more inclined to see knowledge as useful routines that can be learnt for doing things with. Some English or PSE teachers would take another tack, seeing knowledge more as *self*-knowledge, where the 'content' comes from within rather than from outside.

'Of all forms of knowledge, abstract intellectual knowledge and skill are the most important and the most valuable, and success at acquiring them merits a high status and increased choice and earning power in the job market. Being able to solve equations that have no personal relevance; interpret experiments without wondering who first did them; remember the difference between glacial and river valleys; express opinions about books that have not meant much; have conversations in French about your pets with someone you neither know nor trust – these kinds of activities are of importance, certainly more so than the ability to wrestle, to bake, to dive, to meditate, to chat up and to enjoy your own company.'

'It is not important whether the knowledge has direct out-of-school relevance because (1) it is intrinsically worthwhile, and (2) it ought to be automatically generalizable (at least by bright children) to novel appropriate situations. What our abstractions are doing is "training the mind": we are inculcating good habits of thought which will stand people in good stead, regardless of what they end up doing. By detaching the content of learning from the immediate pressures of relevance and need, we are developing valuable general qualities such as rationality.'

'The teacher's job is to present this knowledge, and to train the skills for using or manipulating it, in a way that is clear, well-structured and at an appropriate level and pace.' There are a number of variations on this theme. The teacher may be a *petrol-pump attendant*, whose job it is to fill a child up with high-octane, unleaded knowledge that has been refined elsewhere and delivered to the school by textbook-tankers. (At various times in the year she turns into an *inspector* whose job it is to check for leaks in the child's tank and to see how far he can go on the fuel he has been given.) Teachers of these kinds are inclined to describe their work in terms of 'conveying' or 'imparting' the knowledge, 'getting it across', 'giving a grounding' in whatever-it-is, and so on.

In the same group we might put the *regurgitators*, who see themselves like parent birds who have to take subjects that are too 'tough' and 'chew them over' for pupils so that they will not be too 'hard' for them to 'get their teeth into'. In order to do this, they must see knowledge as something that is created, or at least interpreted, by human beings; but it is their job to do this, not the pupils'. Teachers with all these implicit theories about knowledge must put their energies into seeing that their knowledge is up-to-date and accurate, and that they can deliver it in a clear, well-paced fashion. Good lectures and logical handouts are what they aspire to.

Then there are the *lion-tamers* or the *sculptors*, who see their role in terms of training and moulding. They have a clear idea of what children are to be able to do by the end of their course, and are leading them methodically towards the goal of competence. Children are to be processed, and if they do what they are told to do, and do it 'properly', then they will 'develop' or 'acquire' the target skills. Their focus as teachers is on devising an effective mixture of demonstrations and exercises or 'problems': first they demonstrate how to do it, and then the children practise doing it for themselves. Maths teachers will 'go through it' on the board, answer questions and then offer a kind of coaching service to individuals who get stuck with any of the problems they have been set to do. A similar procedure is familiar in science, where equivalent demonstrations and exercises may be set. As Dennis Fox points out, 'Curiously in science laboratories these exercises are often called "experiments". Anything less like a real scientific experiment, with all its essential uncertainty and unpredictability, would be hard to imagine.'[7] There is not much of a role for the learners' individuality in this model: they lay themselves out on the lathe of the structured, sequenced exercises, and gradually their minds will be turned into the desired shapes.

Next come the *watchmakers*, who see knowledge as a collection of components that have to be assembled in the learners' minds. They often speak of 'building' understanding, frequently using basic ingredients called 'concepts'. There is a grand design, which is usually known to the teacher but not to the learner, and pieces are gradually assembled in the 'right' order. There may be some sense of partnership with the learner in the construction process – after all the building is going on in the learner's mind and she is therefore the only one who has direct access to it – but hers is not to question either the components or the objective. She is to 'grasp' ideas and concepts, and 'make connections' between them.

There are, of course, other ways of looking at the role of the teacher which we shall explore in greater detail later. In particular, we will look at the models of the teacher-as-*sherpa*, acting as a knowledgable local guide to an explorer of unfamiliar terrain; and teacher-as-*gardener*, where all the 'growing' is done by the learner-plants themselves, as they convert nourishment into their own fabric in a way that the gardener can assist, but is powerless to determine. All he can do is arrange the conditions, and then let nature take its course.

'Learners are essentially passive. Their job is to retain or understand knowledge, and to master approved ways of manipulating it.' This assumption underlies, to a greater or lesser extent, all the previous models of teaching bar the last two.

'Learning itself is a pretty simple process which involves adding new bits of information, making connections and developing habits. It has a mechanical rather than an organic feel to it, and the focus of interest is on the process of *teaching* – if we can get the teaching right, then learning will happen as a fairly straightforward consequence. Learning as an activity is engaged and driven by teaching, or at least by good teaching.'

'Learning is something that principally happens in special places – schools – under the guidance and control of special people – teachers. Sure, we might be prepared to admit, when it is drawn to our attention, that children learn to walk, talk, feed themselves and socialize without such an explicitly educational support system; but for *real* learning, the sort that equips you to be a responsible citizen and a rational adult, we need syllabuses, timetables and exams.'

'Not only is abstract intellectual learning the kind that is of most value; learning is itself a primarily intellectual process. It involves mental activities (which so far are treated as unproblematic, remember) like understanding and figuring things out.'

'School learning can therefore be largely disconected from the learners' personalities – provided they are normal and happy. In so far as feelings and emotions are involved at all, a mild level of interest is desirable: we need to be concerned about feelings only when they are getting in the way and gumming up the smooth working of the mind, like treacle poured into an engine. They then constitute a problem to be resolved, so that normal service can be resumed. The solution to this problem should primarily be sought in the learners' own characters, and/or in emotional difficulties that they may be experiencing out of school. When all is going well, personality and emotion can safely be ignored.' (A recently published 'teachers' guide to the psychology of learning', for example, has no entries in its index for *emotion, feeling, personality* or *relationship*.[8])

'Likewise learning is an individual business. It may take place in a social setting – in a sense it must do if a teacher is present – but that merely provides a context for the learning and does not determine, in any qualitative way, the nature of what is learnt. In the right social environment – peaceful, stimulating and supportive – learning will proceed more quickly and smoothly. But as to what is learnt – that is decided by the interaction between the individual learner and the subject matter, with the mediation of the teacher. The meaning of what is to be learnt is inherent in the subject. If groups of learners get together and seek to negotiate the meaning of a lesson or an event, they are likely to wander away from the true meaning – the blind leading the blind.'

'Learning is a homogenous activity, resulting in retention and understanding. It varies not in kind, but in terms of how much or how well the pupils have learnt. And the *processes* whereby we learn are general-purpose: the way we learn does not vary much from subject to subject or context to context. We may do better in one subject than another, but this is a reflection of aptitude, interest or motivation, not of the cognitive approach we take (or of the social relationships between pupils).'

'Once something is learnt "properly", then the "learner" knows it, and unless she "forgets" it she will (should) be able to show that she knows it in the future. Whenever what she knows is actually relevant to a question or a problem, it ought to become available. The idea of relevance, of the ability to see that what was learnt there-and-then is applicable here-and-now, is not problematic: the mind is organized in such a way that, when a piece of knowledge or a mental skill is needed, it automatically pops up like a piece of toast. The odd occasions when this phenomenon of *transfer* does not happen are a nuisance, representing nothing more important than temporary malfunctions of the system. Once it is 'in', there should not be much problem in getting it 'out'. Thus formal examinations provide effective measures of what has been learnt, and generally diagnostic tests of learning or of stage of cognitive development are valid and reliable.'

'Therefore the difficulty with learning lies in acquiring the information. All the weight of our efforts to promote learning must be at the "front end". That is where the problems are to be encountered.'

'Because the main ingredients of this theory are the teacher, the subject matter and the individual learner, it is to these three that we must look for explanations when learning becomes difficult or fails. Perhaps the subject is too difficult, or contains concepts that are too hard. Perhaps the teaching was inadequate: it was confusing or boring or the teacher didn't know his stuff. Or perhaps it is the learner's fault.'

'Learning success is largely determined by two learner variables: ability and effort. Failure to learn usually reflects a deficiency in either or both of these variables – the learner is of low ability or unmotivated.' Actually the reasons that people give for success and failure depend on who they are.[9] Teachers tend to attribute pupils' success mainly to pupil factors such as 'effort' and 'ability' – but also to their own skill as teachers. Failure, on the other hand, is taken to reflect a *lack* of effort or ability, material that is too 'hard', and the good old standby 'home conditions'. Pupils tend to attribute success to their own efforts and abilities, while failure is often put down to lack of parental help and the difficulty of exams. Parents like to take credit for success, but are willing to share it with the teachers; failure is the pupils' 'fault'. Parents are also inclined to use 'home conditions' as an explanation for failure – provided it is clear that it is other people's homes they are talking about.

'When failure is due to lack of effort or ability (as it all too often is) it is personal. It reflects the individual's unwillingness or incapacity to take advantage of what is on offer to all. Both of these – to be thick or not to work hard – are legitimate sources of personal shame. Stupidity and laziness are negative indicators of one's worth.'

'The word "ability", as in "ability level", "high ability", "less able" and so on, denotes a real, personal characteristic which is fixed, limiting, pervasive, predictive, monolithic, measurable and valuable.' 'Fixed' means that it is not subject to significant changes over time, and often is *innately* fixed. 'Limiting' means that the 'ability' people have fixes the upper boundary of what they can achieve and/or the rate at which they can learn. (Other factors such as 'motivation' may prevent a person achieving up to her 'ability level'.) 'Pervasive' means that this limit is operative across the whole range of school subjects, and possibly across the entire cognitive domain. 'Predictive' means that, knowing a person's 'ability', one may predict his future performance. 'Monolithic' means that 'ability' is a simple, coherent thing: it is not composed of many elements. 'Measurable' means that it is possible to discover and quantify 'ability' with the aid of certain diagnostic tests. 'Valuable' means that 'high ability' is better than 'low ability' and that a person's 'ability level' says something important about what she is worth.

THE TRADITIONAL VIEW UNDER PRESSURE

The beliefs that learning was simple, intellectual, cognitive, individual and so on were embedded for many years without question in the way teachers taught and the way schools were organized. Today many of them are the subject of open debate and teachers often feel torn between the different stances towards the business of education that conflicting views seem to imply. On one side there is the Education Reform Act which is built on acceptance of a traditional view of school, strongly based on these beliefs. On the other, there are progressive calls for an education that is concerned with the direct relevance of school activities to young people's ideas, needs and interests. These calls derive from a number of concerns, which teachers often share, such as the changing population of schools and changing attitudes in society at large. Young people are staying on longer at school, and many of them are not going to succeed in the traditional academic subjects. With a high level of youth employment, hard work at school no longer guarantees a 'better job', and young people are less and less inclined to accept respectfully hours of study that seem to them (and to many of their teachers) to have no point or pay-off. Classes contain youngsters from a greater variety of cultural and ethnic backgrounds. Attitudes to the education of girls have changed radically. And so on.

Yet much of the practice in schools continues to be based on the assumptions that were current when the foundations of our school system were being laid a hundred years ago; assumptions that I am going to argue can now be seen to be false. We can no longer assume, for instance, that learning is a single process: rather, different people have different ways of learning, and people have a range of learning styles that they deploy in different situations. We can no longer assume that something learnt in one situation ought automatically to transfer to another: rather, people's knowledge is often tied (and for good reason) to the specific materials and purposes for which they originally learnt it. We can no longer assume that poor performance on a test reflects a failure to 'learn': rather, we have to allow that people may often be unable to retrieve and manifest what they actually do know. We can no longer ignore the experiences and strategies that learners bring into the classroom with them: rather, their idiosyncratic resources influence markedly how, and how well, they learn. We can no longer assume that students' demeanour in class is a reflection of their 'personality' or 'ability': rather, it frequently reflects a rational (though not necessarily conscious) choice about how best to deal with a particular subject or teacher. We can no longer assume that learners' feelings are separable from their mental performance: rather, they are inextricably linked.

As I argued in Chapter 1, the new theory of learning also casts considerable doubt on the validity and even the existence of the construct of 'ability'.[10] The theory suggests that 'ability' may represent only a crude summary of a more complex picture: that learners possess a whole repertoire of learning strategies, some of which are relevant to school but not available (i.e. not copied on to, or cross-referenced with, the 'files' that a learner habitually uses in school); some of which are available and not relevant; and some of which are both available and relevant. It suggests that this repertoire is learnable, and that it can be developed in extent, in refinement and in the success with which the right strategies become available in the right circumstances – circumstances in which their use would actually prove successful. If people's learning power does not develop, this is due not to a 'lack of ability' but to the absence of appropriate experiences, and/or of the emotional or situational conditions which enable those people to explore and extend the current boundaries of their skill as learners. We will explore these conditions later in the book.

LEARNING MEANS AND LEARNING ENDS

What I am going to argue in general is not that the 'traditionalists' have got it all wrong and the 'progressives' have got it all right. What seems obvious to me is that different kinds of learning need to be approached in different kinds of ways. Sometimes there are facts to be learnt and skills to be mastered. I would not want my body to be operated on by someone who did not know the names of the major bones or how to make a clean incision. I am perfectly happy that the person who flies my jumbo jet has been put through thousands of hours of careful training that he or she was probably not consulted about. But equally I do not want the educational psychologist who is called in to help with my daughter's learning problems in school to be trying to sort her out according to some cook-book method. I want him to have developed a warmth and openness when dealing with people that cannot be trained in any mechanical way.

The central questions about school, therefore, are: what kind(s) of learning are we aiming to produce; does everybody involved understand what we are aiming to do, and why; and are we using the right approach for the job? Too often debates about teaching methods are conducted on an antagonistic basis, with a level of subtlety reminiscent of the 'Four legs good; two legs bad' argument in *Animal Farm*.[11] Discovery learning is good, rote learning is bad; free play is good, desk work is bad; experiments are good, note-taking is bad; and so on, as if the issue were a moral and absolute one.

The problem, as I said in Chapter 1, is that you cannot tell whether a learning or teaching method is good or bad until you know the kind of result that is being sought. Teaching styles are *never* good or bad in any absolute sense; they are appropriate or inappropriate. If you want children to know their tables, and to be able to use them spontaneously when they are working with numbers, the best teaching method is the one that delivers –

provided it does not at the same time do any damage to children in other areas of their learning. *If* chanting is efficient and enjoyable, why not use it? Or if you want children to be able to deal successfully with conflict with other people, then rushing in and mopping up every little crisis the minute it occurs may be exactly the least helpful thing to do, despite your own discomfort and hostility. The problem is that people's contributions to educational debates of this sort are frequently expressions of their own implicit theories, derived from happy or unhappy experiences of their own, or their children's, schooldays. They are not open-minded enquiries into the best tool for the job. What are we trying to achieve in education? That is the issue where morals and values are at the heart of the matter. How do we achieve whatever it is we have decided we want? That is a pragmatic question, and the place where psychology can be of help. At *this* stage sentiments and beliefs, however heartfelt, have arrived too late and are merely a nuisance.

If one pitfall that we have to try to avoid is choosing the wrong educational approach for the wrong job, the other is confusing the pupils about what we are doing. It is a frequent source of conflict between pupils or students and teachers when they have differing underlying views about the appropriate way of achieving an educational goal – or even undisclosed disagreements about the goal. There are two classic mismatches. In one, students have the view that the appropriate kind of learning environment is one that involves negotiation, and in which their experience and opinions will be valued and acknowledged. Perhaps they see this as being their 'right', and react to being lectured at or told what to do as if it were an insult. The attitude is not uncommon in undergraduates and teacher training students, especially if they are recently out of school. They feel that being talked at is being treated like a child – the one thing that upsets them more than anything. So for them the issue is not suiting the teaching method to the goal; it is suiting it to the level of maturity of the learners, so that they do not feel 'patronized'. Their teachers and lecturers, however, may see their job more as pump attendants or lion-tamers – and will therefore be constantly faced with learners who seem to them to be stroppy, unappreciative and unwilling to get down to a bit of 'real work'.

Interestingly, the converse mismatch is also alive and well in the teacher training sphere. Here it is the students who are expecting to be given clear information and firm guidelines about how to teach – while the lecturers are asking them to sit down with their eyes closed and reflect on their schooldays, or to engage in classroom role-plays. Here the teachers have a 'gardening' view, in which they see their job as being to provide nurturing soil for the students' own growth, helping them to discover their own beliefs, values and natural strengths. The students, meanwhile, are getting increasingly frustrated as they wait to be sculpted. They are convinced that somewhere there is a detailed blueprint of the British Standard Teacher which is being kept from them for no good reason, and that if only the teachers would stop messing about they could get on with the 'real business' of learning to teach. You can easily tell the lecturers in the two groups, by the way. The former call what they are doing 'teacher training'. The latter are very insistent that it is 'teacher *education*'.

SUMMARY AND READING

People's implicit theories direct their attention, channel their thoughts and limit their actions. This applies as much to their reactions to education as anything else. These theories are often very stable and resistant to change, especially when people may not be aware of what they are explicitly. Making implicit theories explicit is an important precursor to supplanting them with better theories. They derive from three major sources: first-hand experience; informal social interaction and vernacular language; and formal instruction and tuition. Still embedded in the way people think about education, and the way they teach, are a variety of misapprehensions about the nature of learning. Some of these have become the subject of conscious scrutiny and are therefore undergoing change; others are still exercising latent control. This chapter has brought some of these to light in preparation for the challenge to them that the book as a whole represents. There are different ways of learning that deliver different kinds of learning product. This must force educators to specify clearly what kind of goal they are aiming for *before* they enter the debate about appropriate teaching methods.

This chapter has drawn on the growing body of work on people's belief systems and 'folk psychology' that is appearing in the cognitive, educational and especially the social branches of psychology – the latter fuelled largely by the pioneering research in 'attribution theory' of, for example, Bem and Weiner. Rom Harré's *Personal Being* provides an elegant discussion of some of the issues. Paul Heelas and Andy Lock's *Indigenous Psychologies* takes a cross-cultural perspective. And Adrian Furnham's *Lay Theories: Everyday Understanding of Problems in the Social Sciences* is a good introduction which contains a chapter on education. From the educational direction come two strands of research. That on teachers' implicit theories is well represented in *Teacher Thinking*, edited by R. Halkes and J.K. Scott. And work on pupils' implicit theories in the sciences, which raises an exactly parallel set of issues, is critically reviewed in *Pupils' Informal Ideas in Science*, edited by Paul Black and Arthur Lucas. A more technical book in the cognitive sciences tradition is *From Folk Psychology to Cognitive Science: The Case Against Belief* by Steven Stich. Jerome Bruner's recent *Actual Minds, Possible Worlds* also refers to the issue of teachers' beliefs.[12]

NOTES

(1) Axtell, J.L. (ed.) (1968) *The Educational Writings of John Locke*. Cambridge: Cambridge University Press.

(2) Some of these general features of implicit theories of education are reviewed by Dann, H.D. (1986) Reconstruction and validation of teachers' interaction-relevant subjective theories. Paper presented to the Third European Conference on Personality, Gdansk, Poland.

(3) These conditions are clearly spelled out in the context of science teaching by Hewson, P. (1981) A conceptual change approach to learning science. *European Journal of Science Education*, **3**, 383–96.

(4) These terms are used by Driver, R. and Erickson, G. (1983) Theories-in-action: some theoretical and empirical issues in the study of students' conceptual frameworks in science. *Studies in Science Education*, **10**, 37–60; and derive from Argyris, C. and Schon, D. (1974) *Theory in Practice: Increasing Professional Effectiveness*. San Francisco: Jossey-Bass.

(5) In what follows I am drawing heavily on (though going somewhat beyond) a paper by Fox, D. (1983) Personal theories of teaching. *Studies in Higher Education*, **8**, 151–63. I have also made reference to the following: Northedge, A. (1976) Examining our implicit analogies for learning processes. *Programmed Learning and*

Educational Technology, **13**, 67–78; Parsons, J. M., Graham, N. and Honess, T. (1983) A teacher's implicit model of how children learn. *British Educational Research Journal* **9**, 91–101; and Pope, M. L. and Scott, E.M. (1984) Teachers' epistemology and practice. In Halkes, R. and Olson, J. K. (eds), *Teacher Thinking: A New Perspective on Persisting Problems in Education*. Lisse, Holland: Swets & Zeitlinger.

(6)   Feldman, C. and Wertsch, J. (1976) Context dependent properties of teachers' speech. *Youth and Society* **8**, 227–58. This work is referred to by Bruner, J. (1986) *Actual Minds, Possible Worlds*. Cambridge, MA: Harvard University Press.

(7)   See note 5.

(8)   Howe, M. J. A. (1984) *A Teachers' Guide to the Psychology of Learning*. Oxford: Blackwell.

(9)   See research by Bar-Tal, D. and Guttman, J. (1981) A comparison of teachers', pupils' and parents' attributions regarding pupils' academic achievement. *British Journal of Educational Psychology*, **51**, 301–11.

(10)   See, for example, Nisbet, J. (1982) Changing views on ability. *Educational Analysis*, **4**, 1–5.

(11)   George Orwell (1987; original ed. 1945) *Animal Farm*. London: Secker & Warburg.

(12)   For example, Weiner, B. (1985) An attributional theory of achievement, motivation and emotion. *Psychological Review*, **92**, 548–73. Harré, R. (1983) *Personal Being*. Oxford: Blackwell. Heelas, P. and Lock, A. (1981) (eds), *Indigenous Psychologies*. London: Academic Press. Furnham, A. *Lay Theories: Everyday Understanding of Problems in the Social Sciences*. Oxford: Pergamon. Halkes, R. and Scott, J. K. (eds) (1984) *Teacher Thinking: A New Perspective on Persisting Problems in Education*. Lisse, Holland: Swets & Zeitlinger. Black, P. and Lucas, A. (eds) (1990) *Children's Informal Ideas in Science*. London: Routledge. Stich, S. (1983) *From Folk Psychology to Cognitive Science: The Case Against Belief*. Cambridge, MA: MIT Press. Bruner, J. S. (1986) *Actual Minds, Possible Worlds*. Cambridge, MA: Harvard University Press.

Chapter 3

Evolving Models of the Mind

Mind, *n*. A mysterious form of matter secreted by the brain. Its chief activity consists in the endeavour to ascertain its own nature, the futility of the attempt being due to the fact that it has nothing but itself to know itself with.

Ambrose Bierce[1]

Where are we to look for better ideas about learning, ones that avoid some of the distortions and inaccuracies of 'common sense'? The obvious place is in psychology, for it is there that the most sophisticated ideas about the mind and how it works ought to be found. And indeed I am going to show that recent work in psychology, or what has come to be known in the last few years as 'cognitive science', does help us to get a more sensitive grip on what is going on behind the eyes of pupils and students. We need to remember, though, that what we are looking for is not necessarily the most sophisticated theory there is, but one that helps us to think about classroom learning; one that is of practical use. For some purposes the map of the London Underground is more useful than the most detailed, up-to-date Ordnance Survey map.

In order to be able to assess the value of each theory we need to look at it not only from the point of view of its utility, but also in the context of its antecedents and rivals. We need to spend a little time charting the way in which psychological theories of learning have evolved during this century. Learning theories are centrally concerned to answer the question: how is knowledge acquired? (I shall continue to use the word 'knowledge' for the moment not just to refer to intellectual knowledge but to include whatever it is that underlies our skill and personality as well.) But they must also address related questions, such as: how does knowledge interact within the mind; how is knowledge retrieved and expressed; how can learning fail – why is it sometimes difficult, and what happens when we forget; why are people so different in the ease and accuracy with which they learn?

And how is knowledge represented in the mind; how shall we conceive of the structure and organization of knowledge? This last question is the most basic of all. Learning theories concern internal changes in knowledge, and so they must presuppose some model, even if it is only latent, of the nature of the mind itself. Usually we can find, behind each learning theory, a basic metaphor for mind that exerts considerable influence in the way learning is construed. Thus we can explore the evolution of theories of learning in terms of the way these underlying metaphors have changed or been elaborated over the years.

As we track this evolutionary process, so we will be able to see what the models of mind are that have become dissolved in common sense – the impoverished common sense that we laid out explicitly in Chapter 2. Just as common sense views of the workings of the physical world tend to reflect outdated theories in physics, so too are our intuitive psychologies a reflection of technical approaches that have been left behind by the experts in the subject. Approaches to mind and matter alike tend to percolate out of the laboratory into everyday parlance, but at the same time as they are doing so they are being superseded or abandoned by the researchers themselves. And as the diffusion process is a slow one, so the final effect on lay modes of thought is not only simplified, it is out of date.[2]

One of the aims of this chapter, therefore, is to show how these underlying models and images channel and drive the way that questions and answers are formulated about learning. We shall see that, simple though some of these images are, they profoundly affect the 'angle' that is taken and the issues that are brought to the fore or pushed into the background. They make some things easy to see and to talk about, and others hard. A serviceable model of mind is the *sine qua non* for a helpful theory of school learning.

MIND AS WAX

In his book *Theaetetus* Plato outlines two metaphors for mind whose influence has extended into the present century. In the first he likens the mind to wax.

> I ask you to suppose for the sake of argument that we have in our souls a lump of wax for moulding; some a bigger one, some smaller; some of purer and some of impurer wax; some stiffer, some more plastic, and some of average qualities. . . . Let us say . . . that in it, whenever we wish to remember something that we see or hear or think to ourselves, we take an impression, holding it under the sensation or idea, as if we were taking the impression of a seal; and that what is so impressed we remember and know, as long as the outline remains there; and when it is obliterated, or the impression cannot be taken, we forget, or do not know.[3]

Clearly we have here a very passive view of learners: they are just lumps of something that have no say over what happens to them. What an experience means is inherent in the experience; and when it comes along the learner just gets stamped by it. But note that already, even in this brief sketch, we can see the beginnings of explanations for individual differences and for forgetting. Presumably the 'good learner' is someone whose wax is neither too hard (failing to pick up impressions at all) nor too soft (fading away like patterns drawn on a block of butter left in the sun). Unfortunately, however, this simple metaphor leaves the *processes* of learning and retrieval unexplained. There has to be a 'ghostwriter' who does all the interesting work of deciding what impressions to make, and which to read, from moment to moment. It explains very little, and it certainly does not fit with anything we know about how the brain works. Yet taken unreflectively it suggests a model of education based on the rote repetition, the stamping in, of isolated and non-negotiable elements of knowledge.

MIND AS AVIARY

Plato's second image is a more dynamic one.

> Let us now, as it were, frame in each man's soul a dovecote of all manner of birds, some in flocks apart from the others, and some in

small detachments, and some flying about anywhere and everywhere by themselves. . ..When we are children, we must suppose that the receptacle is empty – and by the birds we must understand knowledges; and whatever knowledge is acquired and shut up in the enclosure we must say the child has learned, or has discovered the object to which the knowledge relates; and that this is knowing. Now shall we not compare [remembering] with the possession and recapture of the doves, and say that there was a double chase; one before the acquisition in order to acquire it, and the other after possession, for the purpose of having in his hand what was already long acquired? . . . It is possible for [someone] to have in his hand not the knowledge of the thing he wants, but some other knowledge instead, if, when he is hunting up some particular knowledge from his stock, others fly in the way and he takes one by mistake for another . . . as it were a ringdove instead of a pigeon.[4]

If we compare these two metaphors we can see how different questions are highlighted and different answers suggested. The dovecote suggests some general organization to the mind: how are the birds organized; how are different bits of knowledge arranged with respect to each other; are there basic 'categories' in the mind that correspond to the different sub-compartments of the aviary, and if so what are they? The dovecote suggests that when we forget, it is because we remember the wrong thing, and that this is because the category system is incomplete in some way, so that there remains an element of uncertainty in our search for our memories. And there is also some suggestion that our memories are dynamic; that they can confuse us by changing their 'place'. The wax tablet, on the other hand, suggests that we forget because the original impression has been worn away, or perhaps 'overstamped' with subsequent impressions that have obscured or degraded it. Our experience, as well as psychological research, suggests that we can forget for both these reasons. Sometimes (as in the tip-of-the-tongue feeling) the wrong memory keeps coming to mind even though we know it to be wrong. Sometimes only a faint or distorted record reappears. And sometimes the line is dead and we get no answer at all. Notice that these two models share the idea that knowledge can be treated as separate little pieces; that each little piece has its inherent meaning; and that learning boils down to accumulating more of them. What is different about the second one is that it suggests a role for the teacher in ordering and packaging these pieces in a way that corresponds to the 'natural' compartmentalization of the mind –

into English, science, mathematics, history, geography, French, art and music, for example.

Towards the end of the last century Ebbinghaus initiated the modern study of learning and memory.[5] His approach was very similar to Plato's dovecote. There was a clear distinction between the store (the aviary) and the process of learning and remembering (presumably the disembodied hand grabbing the birds). These processes of putting-in and taking-out were the same whatever size or colour of birds you happen to come across; that is, the processes of learning and retrieval were general-purpose ones which did not depend on the nature or meaning of what you happened to be learning. And (if we rule out reproduction) knowledge was assumed to come in separate pieces that do not interact or integrate with each other. Knowledge is objective. It exists 'out there', and the business of learning is to 'catch' what is out there and to lock it up 'in here'. (Note that the aviary model makes one even more committed to this view of knowledge than the wax tablet model. Someone who has very hard wax may retain only a faint impression, so what people register can vary on a scale of 'more-or-less faithful and vivid'.)

This view of knowledge as objective and atomic led Ebbinghaus to select for his experiments the kind of knowledge that best fitted his preconceptions – small fragments of gibberish that he called 'nonsense syllables', things like 'wef', 'naz' and 'voj'. Having assumed that there were these general learning processes, it made sense to investigate their workings by using 'stimuli' that were as free of prior associations as possible. Meaningful material might arouse memories and feelings which would serve only to cloud the picture. He did a host of experiments (mostly on himself) on memory for these nonsense syllables, and found that the more he had remembered, the harder it was to learn and retrieve new ones (just like the bird-cage: the more there are in there, the harder it will be to get your hands on any particular one). For the first time, but by no means for the last, an experimental psychologist was to select artificial material to be learnt in an artificial task and then to claim that he had discovered entirely general truths about 'the learning mechanism'. This habit, as we shall see, became widely adopted and is one of the main reasons why the application of laboratory models of learning to the classroom has proved to be so fruitless.

MIND AS BATH

As a demonstration of the process of evolution, we could construct a model of mind that combines the 'bird' idea of knowledge as little objects ('facts') with the 'wax' idea that these might change or decay over the course of time. Suppose this time that knowledge is rather like tablets of soap, and that learning involves putting a new one into a bath which may already contain others. Retrieval is trying to find a particular one again. There may now be a number of reasons why memory fails. The soap may have slipped on to the floor rather than into the bath (you failed to 'learn' it). The soap may have dissolved, if it has been sitting in the water for a long time, so that it is no longer there. Or (as is usually the case) it is in there somewhere but you cannot find it (the failure is in retrieval). Using a mnemonic to aid memory is of course analogous to overcoming the problems of soap-retrieval by using soap-on-a-rope. This kind of model was very common in psychology during the 1950s and 1960s. For example, Michael Posner produced a vitriolic version which he called the 'acid-bath' theory.[6] Much experimental research went into trying to pinpoint the main cause of forgetting, but in the end, perhaps because of the simplicity of the underlying metaphor, the issue proved inconclusive and petered out as more sophisticated models were developed.

Notice, however, the effect that such models as this have had on the way in which learning is popularly conceived. The cruder of the implicit theories that we looked at in Chapter 2 can be seen to presuppose some such underlying assumptions, and the emphasis on rote learning and drill that dominated educational practice in the early years of this century derived its justification from them. We have made some progress since then as a result of the shift, attributable most notably in educational circles to Piaget and Bruner, to the more 'cognitive' models of the mind which we shall discuss in a moment.

MIND AS SWITCHBOARD

Alongside the previous kinds of model there developed an approach that was borrowed by students of human learning from their colleagues who were working with animals. The names of

Pavlov and Skinner will probably be familiar to you already. For most of the first half of this century, research into animal learning was dominated by the 'stimulus–response' or S–R framework of behaviourism. Imported into the study of human beings, the stimulus–response idea did at least have the virtue of starting to get away from the stifling assumption that all knowledge consists of separate little nuggets, by providing the most basic kind of association between pieces of knowledge. Instead of learning solely being seen as the accumulation of individual impressions, or 'items' of information, within the switchboard metaphor learning could be seen as the establishing of links between previously unassociated things, so that when one was presented the other tended to be produced as a response. The more frequently and the more recently the two had occurred together, the stronger the link and the more likely each was, when it occured alone, to trigger the other. So memory came to contain simple 'molecules' of knowledge as well as basic 'atoms' of information.

There was another central thread to the behaviourist position, and that was the concern with *skill*, with the development of effective action, in addition to the acquisition of verbal knowledge. This opened the way for education to be seen as training, and for the focus to shift to the problem of establishing the right motivational conditions (positive and negative 'reinforcements') for such learning to happen. Later this was to develop into a more subtle study of the acquisition of skilful competence, but at the time it remained tied to the underlying 'switchboard' model of mental associations which could be strengthened by practice.

As usual, the trouble with this analogy is not so much that it is wrong, as that it works quite well for certain limited *kinds* of learning, like teaching an animal tricks, but it has very little useful to say about how a baby learns language, or how to organize your GCSE revision timetable. It is simply not helpful to try to treat what I know about psychology, for instance, as if it consisted of a heap of mini dumb-bells. I cannot begin to ask any questions that interest me about this area of my knowledge by using this impoverished image.

MIND AS LIBRARY

During the 1960s the metaphors for mind were beginning at last to be interested in its contents. Instead of 'meaning' being seen as something irritatingly idiosyncratic that only served to obscure the workings of the general-purpose learning machine, people gradually came to see that the meaningfulness of information was absolutely central to learning. One development that acknowledged this was that of seeing the mind as a library. Like an elaboration of Plato's sub-compartments of the dovecote, the mind was said to have an intrinsic structure of its own, so that individual pieces of knowledge had a 'place' where they should properly be 'stored'. (The idea of memory as a store came to have such a powerful hold on research during the 1960s and 1970s that it was not seen as a metaphor at all, but as 'obvious' or the 'natural' kind of model.) Learning is putting new things into their 'right place' – like a librarian cataloguing new books. Remembering is searching the shelves. If you were asked to recognize a word from a list, say, or to answer a multiple-choice question, it would be easy because the presented word or suggested answer gives you its 'call-mark' so that you can go straight to the right place and see (1) if the book is there, and (2) if it is, whether it has been 'taken out' recently. If the answer is 'yes' to both, you recognize it. If it is 'no' to either, you do not.

But if you are asked to *recall* a list of words, that would be harder because you do not know so precisely where to look. If you are lucky and the test comes quickly on the heels of the learning, you might find some of the books still on the 'recent returns' rack waiting to be reshelved. Or knowing the *kind* of word you are looking for might help if the category corresponds to the way the library is organized. Underwood, for example, argued that there are a number of basic dimensions along which the mind as a whole is organized. Others preferred a general hierarchical 'tree' structure, with very abstract categories like 'thing' at the top, progressing down through 'living thing', 'animal', 'mammal', 'canine', 'dog', 'terrier' and 'fox terrier' to 'Billie, the fox terrier next door'.[7]

This soon came to look too neat, however. It did not seem as if the mind conveniently constrains itself to just a few obligatory principles of organization, but that it retains the flexibility to organize itself along the lines that make the most sense in terms of the subject that it happens to be learning. Here, for the first time, we are beginning to see the realization that what goes on in the mind might be dependent on the particular kind of knowledge with which it is dealing. We could start to model this with a less regimented version of the library – the kitchen. In one's own kitchen the organization is less conceptual and more functional. You can keep the garlic, grated Parmesan and oregano together on a shelf by the cooker (and not with the rest of the herbs and spices) if you are going through a pasta phase. It does not matter if you keep the grater under the sink and the lemon-juice squeezer in with the cat food: if the system works for you, that is enough. It does not have to be neat so long as it is *familiar*, and is *relevant* to your needs and interests. With this move, therefore, we can introduce considerations of habit and motivation to offset the previously overriding assumption that the mind must be organized generally, elegantly and economically.

MIND AS COMPUTER: FIRST VERSION

As we noted in passing just now, libraries (and kitchens), as well as having long-term storage, also have smaller, more flexible stores for recently returned or acquired books that have not yet been filed and indexed, or for shopping that has not yet been put away in its correct place. In the 1960s there was much concern with the characteristics of the mental equivalent – 'short-term memory' as it was called. At first short-term memory (STM) was seen as a temporary place to park newly arrived information until it could be properly processed ('encoded') in terms of its meaning. That was how learning was conceived: it was like putting away the shopping, thinking to yourself 'Now . . . flour . . . where does that live? Ah, that's right: behind the tinned fruit.' STM was assumed to have a quite general function, so that its capacity, and the form ('code') in which information was held, were inherent characteristics of the store and did not depend on what in particular was being temporarily housed within it – just as your kitchen worktop will only hold so much shopping, regardless of what it is. Things might be easier to file (learn) than others if they are more common. It takes longer to remember, or figure out, where the birthday cake candles are kept than it does the washing-up liquid.

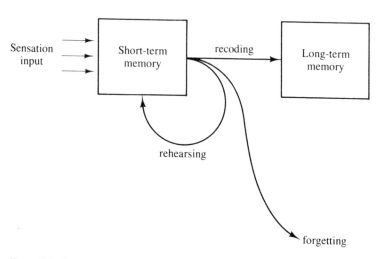

Figure 3.1. Short-term and long-term memory.

The Ebbinghaus assumption of general-purpose mechanisms was retained and strengthened within this model by linking it with an analogy between mind and computer. The digital computer was still a relatively new device at the time, and one of its most obvious characteristics was the distinction between a large, passive 'long-term memory' (LTM) store and the small-capacity, active 'central processor' or 'accumulator', which was the only place where newly arrived information and information retrieved from LTM could meet and interact. There was an obvious link to be made between this general-purpose, limited-capacity central processor and STM. Learning thus came to be seem as processing new inputs in STM (or 'working memory', as it came to be known in the 1970s) and then transferring them to a storage location in LTM. Forgetting could result from two causes: either information is lost from STM before it has been 'processed' (like the dog stealing the meat from the counter before you have a chance to put it in the fridge), or it is lost somewhere in LTM (like those candles that you have not used for a year – or the soap in the bath, to revert to an earlier image).

Research within this tradition has continued into the 1980s,[8] but the metaphor is now much less popular than it was twenty years ago, and has been the subject of considerable criticism.[9] The distinction between STM and LTM was nevertheless a classic example of a psychological idea that filtered through into the folklore of educational psychology, where it remains, in a simplified and archaic form, enshrined in the most popular text-books.[10] Wild generalizations are still made. For example, because tests showed that STM could 'hold' only seven digits, more or less, teachers and lecturers are sometimes told to be sure not to make more than seven points per lesson.[11]

MIND AS NET

The 'kitchen' principle was investigated during the 1970s by a major research effort focusing on modelling the detailed structure of LTM, rather than trying to discover general characteristics of its organization. This research relied extensively on a metaphor that was essentially an elaboration of the association idea. Instead of links between the 'meaning atoms' being of only one kind, and only between pairs of atoms, now the mind was allowed to contain multiple kinds of link, so that ideas are woven together into large, complex networks (for example, see Figure 3.2). 'Semantic memory', as it came to be called, was imagined to be like a large tangled fishing net, through which paths could be traced from one idea to another.

The question of how these paths are traced (as, for example, in answering GCSE questions that require you to use your accumulated knowledge to solve novel kinds of problem) could be answered in two ways. In the first there was supposed to be a separate kind of memory ('procedural knowledge') that consists of rules and 'programs' for controlling the search of the inherently passive network of information ('declarative knowledge'). The distinction was like that between the 'program-store' and the 'database' of a computer,[12] or perhaps between the librarian and the library. In the alternative model, the net itself is made of 'wires' along which activation of some kind can flow, 'lighting up', as it were, ideas and concepts as it goes, and, by making them concurrently active, allowing new links and implications to be seen. At each 'junction' in the network the relative 'resistance' of the possible onward paths determine which direction the

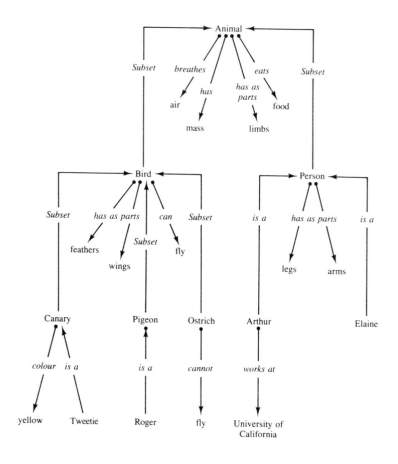

Figure 3.2. A simple part of a semantic network.

activation will take.[13] In both of these types of model, ideas or concepts were represented as local 'fragments' of the network that contain essential information about definitions and associations.

This kind of model fits well with the idea of teaching as 'developing concepts', 'making conections' and 'building bridges'; and learning begins to look a more variegated and a more interesting business. We can immediately see three ways in which the knowledge contained by this system, and therefore its behaviour, could be changed. The first involves developing the network, either by adding on new pieces of information at its edges, like a spider enlarging its web, or by discovering more links between ideas already within it, like the spider filling in gaps to make its web stronger. In the second there is the possibility of developing new 'programs' that can manipulate knowledge ('solve problems') in new ways. This kind of learning, derived from this kind of underlying picture, is popular now in the 'skills' approach to education in science or history, for example. And thirdly (echoes of the old 'switchboard' idea, but now in a more wide-ranging context) one might be capable of altering the 'resistance' of links and gates in the network of pathways, so that activity ('the train of thought') will flow in different directions. And 'concepts' can now be visualized not as atoms of meaning, but as perhaps quite complicated collections of more basic ideas and associations bound together by the links. The mind begins to look rather more 'real' in this picture, like a huge multi-dimensional dictionary of information cross-referenced in millions of ways.

MIND AS DICTIONARY/DIARY

Models of 'semantic memory', however, were unable on their own to account for all of human learning. For in addition to changing our concepts, we also obviously remember events. We have a record – albeit a patchy one – of our own autobiography. So as well as a 'dictionary' kind of memory, we also keep a mental 'diary'. Tulving proposed that, in addition to semantic memory, we also have an 'episodic memory' for recording our lives.[14] Each moment we are inscribing a new entry in the diary, but in order to do so, to make sense of what is going on, we have to keep drawing on the conceptual generalizations stored in the dictionary.

As the relationship between the dictionary and the diary was explored experimentally, the long-standing assumption that the mind's ideas are atomic came under even more severe attack. When words are used together in phrases and sentences, the ideas referred to do not just stand side by side: they typically interpenetrate and coalesce, so that the meaning of each is modified and shaped by the presence of the others. For example, if I describe someone as 'generous to a fault' or as 'hot and bothered', what you understand is not just the meanings of 'generous' and 'fault' or of 'hot' and 'bothered' added together. We choose a *shade* of meaning of each, one which best fits with the context provided by its partner. Take an example of a sentence that is not easy, on first acquaintance, to understand, like 'The notes were sour because the seams split'.[15] We do not merely assemble a pile of the meanings of the individual words and leave it at that. Rather we treat it like a puzzle which, if we could only get each of the pieces the right way round, would fit together much more satisfyingly. Given the clue 'bagpipes', most people are able to find a sense of 'sour', albeit an unusual, metaphorical one, which will do the job.

Understanding thus becomes the business of *creative modification* of what we know, and is not merely constructing links, however fine, between independent elements of thought. It is more like baking a cake than building with Lego. Such analogies as this led to the idea, still current today, that concepts are typically not well-defined but fuzzy, with some central features and an array of optional extensions which can be selected in different contexts. Learning becomes a matter of exploring these extensions so that the customized selection can be made, for each concept, which seems to make the best, most integrated overall sense of a situation.[16]

Notice that we have now reached a point, as a result of the gradual evolution of these models of mind, where the prior experience of the learner is playing an absolutely crucial role in channelling the understanding that she derives from her experience. She is now drawing on her store of associations and connotations to every idea she comes across in order to make sense of it in her own terms. Meaning is no longer cut and dried, neatly packaged in an idea or a formula that one person can give to another. Rather on this view meaning is always something that people make. It is as if the best anyone else can do is to give us an outline sketch, and it is then up to us in what way, and to what extent, we flesh it out and colour it in.

MIND AS COMPUTER: SECOND VERSION

Apart from a concern with the personal and flexible nature of learning, another shift in thinking has occured in the last ten years or so. This is away from global, monolithic models towards a view that sees the mind as comprising a collection of sub-minds, each of which is specialized for dealing with a particular area of experience, or a particular kind of task. This amounts to rejection of the Ebbinghaus assumption of 'pure' processes that can apply to any relevant subject matter. Instead there is some agreement now that, as Allport put it in the title of his 1980 book chapter, 'cognitive mechanisms are content-specific'.[17] Some authors see these sub-minds as being still quite general.[18] Gardner, for example, puts forward the idea that we possess not one unitary 'intelligence' but seven quite separate intelligences, specialized for learning about music, physical skills, logic and mathematics, language, spatial relationships, interpersonal relationships and self-knowledge. While this seems to echo the old idea of the library, having separate sections, the improvement is that he is talking not merely about different kinds of knowledge, but about different ways of thinking, learning and operating.

Other people have argued that our minds may be divided up into much smaller 'intelligences' than this, and that they consist essentially of purpose-built 'frames', 'scripts' or 'minitheories' that are designed to cope with familiar scenarios.[19] It is models of this type that I am going to elaborate in Chapter 4.

THE MAJOR CHANGES

Let us just take stock for a moment and review some of the major trends and changes in this revolutionary process. First, there has been a shift from thinking of discrete bits of knowledge to looking at the way that knowledge is integrated and tied up together. Second, because of these interconnections, we now see 'concepts' as being, in general, ill-defined rather than clear-cut. Each concept may have a 'core of meaning', but it also has a lot of trails and associations that can be followed up if the situation calls for it. Recently, for example, Rumelhart and McClelland have developed a new family of models, called 'parallel distributed processing' or PDP models, that are based much more closely on what we know about the structure and function of the human brain.[20] These use the idea that we introduced above of a flow of activity through a network, but instead of using clearly defined links between 'concepts', represented as points or nodes in the network, concepts are now seen as a loose affiliation of many more elementary units that may be scattered quite widely throughout the network as a whole. Instead of a coarse net, the mind is a pile of very fine mesh. Such distributed patterns certainly seem to correspond more closely to the way the brain is organized. These models are causing considerable excitement in cognitive science at the moment, but it is too early to tell whether their degree of detail will turn out to be of help to people in education trying to understand classroom learning.

Third, people are now more interested in the *processes* of learning and thinking and less concerned with trying to carve the mind up into major structural components like LTM and STM. Fourth, there is a feeling that particular processes or operations may be tied more closely than we had previously supposed to certain kinds of mental job or physical situation. The idea that there is one general kind of memory for knowledge ('knowing that') and another for skill ('knowing how')[21] seems to be giving way to the idea of a large collection of more purpose-built programs or files, each of which (or groups of which) may be 'formatted' or organized in the way that suits its (their) function best. Thus there may not be a single kind of organization that applies to all our areas of knowledge and expertise. Fifth, this way of looking at the mind opens up the question of the different programs or strategies that people may possess, and that may become available in the same or different situations.

The sixth shift involves a major expansion of the kinds of learning we can think about. The older metaphors led us to think of learning as adding new knowledge to a store that was expanded thereby. But now we can see ways of talking about other kinds of learning, such as tuning or modifying what we already know, restructuring pre-existing files in the light of new experience, or even deleting or superseding things that we have found out to be inaccurate or false.[22] As we shall see later, these kinds of learning are extremely relevant to an understanding of what is actually going on in the classroom. In general we are also led to think of learning very much as changes in process, in the *way* we think and learn, as well as changes in the content of *what* we know.

The seventh shift is an important one too. In the newer models the process of learning can take place only through the use of what we already know. The mind's existing stock of files is what is used in order to make sense of new experience. So it follows that the sense that people make is completely dependent on the knowledge they have already accumulated, and on which parts of that are brought to bear on the problem of deciding what is going on, and what to do about it. We perceive and learn with our minds, and the learning that we do is constructed by our minds.

This general approach to the mind we referred to in Chapter 2 as *constructivism*, and it is in stark contrast to the empiricist alternative which sees learning as the more-or-less accurate recording of knowledge that exists objectively, outside the learner. In the constructivist view, learning is a personal and an active process. It is personal because we can understand or retain new things only in terms of the pre-existing knowledge that we bring to the learning situation. And learning is active because it is only through the purposeful mobilization of this store of knowledge that new knowledge or skill can come about. We have no other place to stand, in order to comprehend the world, than on the platform of our own current knowledge.

While our minds may well contain some elementary processes and links, as suggested by the earlier metaphors, especially when we are very young, they come to contain much more complexity. In particular, we acquire the ability to represent what we know in a variety of different formats, so that the same event, depending on how it is processed, can come to have quite different internal repercussions. And also, as we grow up, we not only learn more, but we learn how to learn. Just as our inner theories grow in extent and complexity, so too does the tool-kit of learning strategies on which we can draw to build these mental models.

SOME ILLUSTRATIVE EVIDENCE

These changes in our view of learning have come about for a number of different reasons, some empirical, some concerning the kinds of problem that computer scientists have been forced to face as they have tried to write programs that mimic some aspects of the structure and function of the human mind, and some for more philosophical reasons. Let me just give a few examples of some of the experimental work that has helped to bring about the shift.

There is now considerable evidence for the idea that available properties of the mind vary from problem to problem and from context to context. Margaret Donaldson and her associates have shown with younger children how their apparent abilities depend markedly on the way in which a particular problem is phrased.[23] If the content of the problem is familiar and meaningful to them, they are more likely to be able to bring their reasoning skills to bear than if it is not – even though the logical demand of the problems is the same. Thus dramatic changes in children's apparent ability can be brought about by changing what may seem to be quite trivial or incidental features of a problem situation.

Take the classic 'conservation of number' problem, for example where 6-year-olds reliably say that a row of beads has become 'less' when they are bunched up rather than spread out. Now make one small modification: instead of the 'experimenter' solemnly shifting the beads about, a toy character called 'Naughty Teddy' appears and 'messes them up'. Suddenly the children are under no illusions about what this has done to the *number* of beads on the table – nothing. When the change seems to result from an 'accident' – a kind of event with which children are very familiar – they are able to tell what has 'really' changed and what has not. But when an adult *deliberately* makes a difference to the way something looks – that is a different matter, one where children are less sure-footed and have to fall back on trying to infer what the grown-ups are doing. The problem is then more of a social than a cognitive one: 'what does this stranger want me to say?' And most 6-year-olds, not surprisingly, make the wrong bet.[24]

Again consider the situation, if anything even more classic, of 'conservation of volume', the one where orange juice is poured from a short fat beaker into a tall thin tube, and the 6 and 7-year-olds say that it has become 'more'. Simply embed this unfamiliar operation within a meaningful scenario about a giraffe who cannot bend down to drink and a hippo who cannot reach up, and the children are quite happy that the pourings between containers leave them with the same amount of juice.[25] It is as if, with younger children especially, abilities are first developed within a particular 'file' so that, unless that file is accessed by the problem, the requisite ability is not available. Only later in development do these abilities begin to get 'disembedded' and to become more widely accessible.

But the effect of situation-dependency is by no means confined to primary schoolers. Here are a couple of examples from the context of science in the secondary school. One of the questions set by the Assessment of Performance in Science Unit, which is trying to monitor just what pupils have learnt in their science lessons, asked them to solve two similar problems that involved deducing which of a number of possible 'agents' were responsible for the sickness of some hypothetical children.[26] They were given pieces of information like 'Mary and Jane did not eat the ice-cream' and had to combine them to find out which did what to whom. In one version of the problem, the potential 'culprits' were all types of food. In the other, they were different children (so the question was 'who had the measles, and who gave it to whom?'). These two versions were supposed, by the researchers, to be equivalent, and simply to act as a check for each other. But the results showed that the 'food' version was solved reliably better than the 'other children' one. Moreover, when the pupils were asked to justify their answers, 27 per cent of the answers to the food problem 'imported' beliefs and information that were additional to the information presented in the test, while for the children problem only 2 per cent of answers showed such gratuitous additions. Why? Because the characters in the children story – Simon, Jill, Karen, Tamsin and their friends – are unknown to the problem-solvers, whereas they have extensive first-hand experience of the sickness-making properties of the different 'characters' in the food problem – ice-cream, hot-dogs, chips, toffee-apples and so on. When a problem hooks into personal experience, then that experience, and the lessons it has taught us, are mobilized in the search for a solution. As we shall see, this can sometimes be a hindrance as well as a help. But it is what happens.

The second example[27] shows the crucial effect of how we, as teachers, even choose our words. Pupils were told that two equal amounts of water were poured together and they were asked to state the temperature of the mixture. In the case where the contributions were described as 'two lots of cold water', the pupils rightly responded that the temperature of the mixture would be 'the same'. But when the problem was phrased in terms of 'two lots of water each at 10 degrees Celsius' there was a marked tendency to say that the temperature of the mixture would be 20 degrees. The presence of numbers in the problem caused them to

switch from their (appropriate) lay theory of hot and cold, which
made their experience available to them, to a 'sums' program that
was out of place, and that led them to produce answers which were
not referred back to 'common sense'.

Interestingly, some pupils, when confronted with the apparent
conflict between their two answers, continued to side with the
number theory and changed their (originally correct) answer to the
first problem, saying, 'Oh, it must be *twice as cold.*' This, of
course, gets them even further into hot (or cold) water because the
formula they are using, which is 'twice x', gives different answers
when x = 'cold' and when x = '10 degrees'. The 'cold' water gets
colder; the '10 degree' water gets hotter! Yet this is rarely spotted
by the pupils because they are switched into a way of operating
which delivers solutions to 'sums', not real predictions about
physical events. This kind of behaviour will come as no surprise to
teachers, especially of maths, who are used to the phenomenon of
pupils apparently jettisoning their common sense when faced with
'school learning'.

SUMMARY AND READING

This chapter has presented a review of psychological models of the
mind and its functioning, highlighting the way in which they have
first provided the substrate for implicit, lay theories of learning
and teaching, and have then moved beyond common sense to a
more differentiated and integrated view that needs now to become
the 'common knowledge' that guides educational thinking.
Specifically, the mind is now viewed by many researchers in
psychology and cognitive science as a vast assemblage of partially
interconnected but also partially autonomous 'scripts', 'frames' or
'minitheories' that provide the wherewithal for perception,
understanding and learning, and that are, in their turn, modified
by tuition and experience. The shifts in the view of the mind that
have led to this current picture include seeing knowledge as more
integrated, less atomistic; more fine-grained and fuzzy, less clearly
definable and molar; more mutable and provisional, less rigid and
objective; more situation-specific, less general-purpose; more
process and content together, less separation between knowing
how and knowing that. We have noted one or two issues that these

changes raise for the understanding of learning, though the major exploration of these implications will come later in the book. And we have looked at some experimental results of children's problem-solving in a range of contexts that illustrate some of the reasons why these shifts have taken place.

Clearly these developments have involved much more detailed argument than I have been able to recapitulate here, and there is also much current controversy, as you would expect, to which I have not done justice. The tension between general-purpose and content-specific views of cognition is not resolved: they are revealed in the contributions to my edited collection, *Growth Points in Cognition*, and to the collection edited by Graham Davies and Donald Thomson, *Memory in Context: Context in Memory*.

This chapter has focused on cognitive models and has had little to say about emotion, social relationships, personality or culture. I am coming to these, but there are people who would argue with the emphasis implied by the order. *Changing the Subject* by J. Henriques and others insists that the social is primary, and would consider that, by taking an essentially, 'individualistic' stance, I have already begged the most important educational and cultural issues – as indeed would much of the work of the modern sociologists of education, such as Hammersley and Woods.[28]

NOTES

(1)   Ambrose Bierce (1958) *The Devil's Dictionary*. Toronto: Dover.
(2)   See Churchland, P. (1979) *Scientific Realism and the Plasticity of Mind*. Cambridge: Cambridge University Press, for an account of how this transformation of expert into public knowledge happens in the physical and biological sciences. McClosky, M. (1983) Intuitive physics. *Scientific American*, **248**, 114–22, gives a comparison of children's understanding of physics with the scientists' picture.
(3)   Carlill, H. F. (1906) *The Theaetetus and Philebus of Plato*. London: Swan Sonnenschein, p. 68.
(4)   Ibid., pp. 76–8.
(5)   Ebbinghaus, H. (1885) *Über das Gedächtnis*. Leipzig: Duncker.
(6)   Posner, M. I. (1967) Short-term memory systems in human information processing. *Acta Psychologica*, **27**, 267–84.
(7)   Underwood, B. J. (1969) Attributes of memory. *Psychological Review*, **76**, 559–73. Bower, G. H., Clark, M., Lesgold, A. and Winzenz, D. (1969) Hierarchical retrieval systems in the recall of

categorised word lists. *Journal of Verbal Learning and Verbal Behavior*, **8**, 323–43.

(8)   See, for example, Halliday, M.S. and Hitch, G. (1988) Developmental applications of working memory. In Claxton, G.L. (ed.) *Growth Points in Cognition*. London: Routledge.

(9)   For instance, Allport. D. A. (1980) Patterns and actions: cognitive mechanisms are content-specific. In Claxton, G. L. (ed.) *Cognitive Psychology: New Directions*. London: Routledge & Kegan Paul.

(10)   For example: Child, D. (1986) *Psychology and the Teacher*, 4th edn. London: Holt, Rinehart & Winston; Fontana, D. (1988) *Psychology for Teachers*, 2nd edn. Leicester: British Psychological Society/Macmillan; Tomlinson, P. (1981) *Understanding Teaching: Interactive Educational Psychology*. London: McGraw-Hill.

(11)   For example, Bligh, D. (1972) *What's the Use of Lectures?* Harmondsworth: Penguin.

(12)   See Anderson, J. R. (1983) *The Architecture of Cognition*. Cambridge, MA: Harvard University Press.

(13)   Collins, A. M. and Loftus, E. F. (1975) A spreading activation theory of semantic processing. *Psychological Review*, **82**, 407–28.

(14)   Tulving, E. (1972) Episodic and semantic memory. In Tulving, E. and Donaldson, W. (eds), *Organisation of Memory*. New York: Academic Press.

(15)   Anderson, R. C. and Ortony, A. (1975) On putting apples into bottles: a problem in polysemy. *Cognitive Psychology*, **7**, 167–80.

(16)   Smith, E. E. and Medin, D. L. (1981) *Categories and Concepts*. Cambridge, MA: Harvard University Press. Tulving, E. (1983) *Elements of Episodic Memory*. Oxford: Oxford University Press. For a fuller discussion of this issue, see Claxton, G. L. (1984) *Live and Learn: An Introduction to the Psychology of Growth and Change in Everyday Life*. London: Harper & Row, chapter 4; reissued (1988), Milton Keynes: Open University Press.

(17)   See note 9.

(18)   Fodor, J. A. (1983) *The Modularity of Mind*. Cambridge, MA: MIT Press. Gardner, H. (1983) *Frames of Mind*. New York: Basic Books.

(19)   Minsky, M. (1988) *The Society of Mind*. London: Pan. Schank, R. and Abelson, R. (1977) *Scripts, Plans, Goals and Understanding*. Hillsdale, NJ: Erlbaum.

(20)   Rumelhart, D. E. and McClelland, J. L. (1986) *Parallel Distributed Processing: Explorations in the Microstructure of Cognition*. Cambridge, MA: MIT Press.

(21)   Ryle, G. (1949) *The Concept of Mind*. London: Hutchinson.

(22)   Rumelhart, D. E. and Norman, D. A. (1978) Accretion, tuning and restructuring: three modes of learning. In Cotton, J. W. and Klatzky, R. L. (eds), *Semantic Factors in Cognition*. Hillsdale, NJ: Erlbaum.

(23)   Donaldson, M. (1978) *Children's Minds*. London: Fontana. Donaldson, M., Grieve, R. and Pratt, C. (eds) (1983) *Early*

Childhood Development and Education. Oxford: Blackwell.
(24) See Donaldson, *Children's Minds*, op. cit.
(25) This effect was demonstrated by Maggie Mills of Bedford College London (as it then was) in a Thames Television series of programmes on psychology called *All in the Mind*. See the book: Nicholson, J. and Lucas, M. (eds) (1984) *All in the Mind*. London: Methuen.
(26) Russell, T. (1985) Interpreting presented information. In *APU Report No 4: Science in the Schools, Age 11*. London: Department of Education and Science.
(27) Strauss, S. and Stavy, R. (1983) Educational–developmental psychology and curriculum development: the case of heat and temperature. In Helm, H. and Novak, J. D. (eds), *Proceedings of the International Seminar on Misconceptions in Science and Mathematics*. Ithaca, NY: Cornell University Press.
(28) Claxton, G. L. (ed.) (1988) *Growth Points in Cognition*. London: Routledge. Davies, G. M. and Thomson, D. M. (eds) (1988) *Memory in Context: Context in Memory*. Chichester: Wiley. Henriques, J., Holloway, W., Urwin, C., Venn, C. and Walkerdine, V. (1984) *Changing the Subject*. London: Methuen. Hammersley, M. and Woods, P. (eds) (1984) *Life in School: The Sociology of Pupil Culture*. Milton Keynes: Open University Press.

Chapter 4

Minitheories

Though analogy is often misleading, it is the least misleading thing we have.

Samuel Butler[1]

In Chapters 2 and 3 I have tried to lay the ground for an improved understanding of learning in schools; one that goes beyond the constraints of unreflective common sense and the limitations of out-of-date psychologies. As an introduction to what is to follow, let me point up three of the main considerations to have emerged.

First, the mind is organized into localized packages that are tied to particular kinds of familiar situation, and that do not make a functional distinction between knowledge-as-content and knowledge-as-skill or process. The fundamental principle in terms of which the mind is ordered is not 'what is it?', but 'what is it *for*?'. This approach raises the problem of how we are to conceive of such a mind; how we are to think about it and the way it works.

It also highlights perhaps the biggest issue that education has to face: how to teach in such a way that what is learnt becomes available subsequently when it is needed. The assumption has long been that what is learnt in school will be portable – it can readily be carried out of the school gates and applied to 'real life' – but this now appears questionable. Of course, there is some interaction between what is learnt in school and what is learnt outside. But competencies that are acquired in the context of one school subject seem very often not even to transfer over to other subjects, let alone out-of-school contexts. It has begun to look as if our capabilities are always born within a particular context of opportunity and intent, and that it requires additional learning for those birth-ties to be weakened or broken. If we want education to be a preparation for living, as well as an induction into valued forms of knowledge within our culture, then this problem of 'disembedding' has to be tackled.

Second, traditional approaches to school learning, especially but not exclusively at the secondary level, have focused on the acquisition of various kinds of intellectual knowledge and the skills of manipulation that go with them. They aim to teach pupils to write and to use different 'voices' in their writing; to read fluently and for different purposes; to retain what they have been shown or told and to recapitulate it accurately; to hold rational and productive discussions; to master the rudiments of languages other than their own; to use the special kind of language called 'mathematics' and 'chemistry'; to develop rational explanations for natural phenomena; and so on. The assumption has clearly been that education is mainly about accumulating areas of mental expertise, and that the process of accumulation is predominantly a cognitive one.

Now if we have deliberately *chosen* intellectual knowledge as the most relevant and valuable for all our young people to acquire; have rationally decided that it is this above everything else that will equip them all to function well in the first years of the next millennium; and have done so in the conscious light of the total range of other learning options that are available, and that we have therefore deliberately downgraded – then that is fine. But if, as I believe, this emphasis on the intellectual, competitive nature of school was the result not of an informed decision, recurrently reviewed in the light of the freshest and best available expert opinion (about learning, for example), but of a misplaced reverence for tradition, a sense of inertia and an apparent lack of alternatives to think about, then this 'new psychology of learning' might well remind us of learning possibilities that we have forgotten: possibilities that may be more attainable, and more appropriate, at the end of the twentieth century than they were at the beginning. And it might also raise questions about the extent to which the activities of learning can be decoupled from the concerns, feelings and beliefs of the person as a whole.

Third, our analysis has raised the possibility of learning how to learn. I believe that the prime function of education in an uncertain world should be to provide young people with the competence and self-confidence to tackle uncertainty well; in other words, to be good learners. Recent work on learning strategies has made it possible for us to see much more clearly what exactly this means, and what conditions serve to foster or to inhibit the development of good learners. I shall take this up in Chapter 5, along with an examination of the aspects of learning that are predominantly intellectual. In this chapter I shall concentrate on the other main issue: how to describe, and to educate, a 'modular' mind. We shall also run into the question of the extent to which school learning *is* an individual, intellectual process.

THE MODULAR MIND

The basic idea that I am going to develop is that our knowledge consists of a large number of purpose-built, situation-specific packages called 'minitheories', and that our basic method of learning – our *natural learning ability*, as I shall call it – involves a gradual process of editing these minitheories so that they come (1) to contain better-quality knowledge and skill, and (2) to be better 'located' with respect to the area of experience for which they are suitable. I want to start by introducing some simple analogies that will help us to think in these ways, and then to get a little more technical in order to draw out some of the implications for education. The images I shall use vary in a variety of ways, but they all share the same fundamental characteristics.

Islands

The first analogy is that of islands in an ocean. The sea represents everything we do not know, and the islands are the aspects of life that we more or less understand. When a new experience occurs on one of our islands we are 'on firm ground': we have a reasonable idea what kind of a thing it is and how to go about dealing with it. When it falls in the water we are more 'at sea', and we do not have such a clear idea what is going on, or how to behave. When things are in shallow water, a little strange perhaps, but close to the borders of our competence, we can explore off the coast, paddle about, build bridges and piers and so on. Investigation is relatively easy, and we can, if necessary, redraw the boundaries of our island according to what we discover. Learning is reclaiming dry land from the sea. This is the natural learning ability.

When things occur that are more unfamiliar, then we find ourselves 'out of our depth', and we need other *learning strategies* (like swimming or boat-building) if we are to embark on the learning course. Mostly when things occur far out at sea we can afford to ignore them. But sometimes we have to face up to them and do what we can – even though we are very unsure how to proceed.

Sometimes islands grow together and link up as we realize that two originally separate domains are actually, below the surface, just variations on a common theme. And sometimes an island will split in half as we explore it more fully; we realize that we have failed to make a distinction that is actually quite important, and we discover two sub-domains that are better treated as different.

Amoebae

The second analogy is similar to the first, but gives the sense that learning is a more dynamic, more responsive process. Here the different minitheoris are like amoebae lying on a flat surface. Each amoeba represents one of our packages of competence, and, like the islands, its location and outline on the surface correspond to the domain of experience to which it currently applies. Within its form lie events that we believe we can handle, using the resources that that particular amoebic package happens to provide. As learning occurs, so the 'skills' and 'knowledge' of an amoeba increase; but also it shifts its position and shape so that it comes, more and more, to lie over that portion of the surface with which it successfully deals. When this has happened, it is not called up to cope with events that actually lie outside its range of competence; nor does it fail to respond to events about which it *can* provide appropriate advice. When something occurs that lies beyond the current borders of any amoeba, the one that considers itself (perhaps after a consultation with some of the other candidates) the 'nearest' will tentatively stick out a pseudopodium (one of its expandable legs) to 'cover' the unfamiliar occurrence and see if the event can be subsumed under its auspices.

Computer files

The third analogy likens the minitheories to the different files in a computer – the different documents stored by a word processor, let us say. I have hinted at this metaphor already, towards the end of Chapter 3. You might imagine that the mind contains thousands of 'files', each with its own information and its own sphere of relevance. Files may contain cross-references to each other, and may also have their own sub-routines for doing particular jobs. They must also have names, and perhaps 'search paths', which enable you to tell what is in them and how to get to it. Learning, in this metaphor, involves adding to or modifying the 'programs' in a file; creating new files to deal with novel kinds of situation; and refining the 'indexing' of the disks and files so that one comes to select more reliably the best available program to deal with the current situation. One particularly useful feature of this approach is the idea that learning itself involves the running of particular programs, those that we have called 'learning strategies'. This conceptualization highlights the possibility that these strategies are themselves learnt and subject to further modification.

HEADs and TALEs

The final image I want to be able to use is the hardest to explain, in the sense that it is custom-built rather than an off-the-peg analogy like the other three. It is also the most specific: it goes into more detail about the internal structure of minitheories. Sometimes this level of detail will be necessary in order to understand something about learning, but often we do not need to be so precise and one of the other three will do perfectly well. You might imagine that this fourth image, of what I shall call *modules*, represents a higher power of magnification. If you put a minitheory under a microscope, so as to look at its structure more carefully, this is what you will see. (There are more detailed levels of analysis still, such as that provided by the 'parallel distributed processing' models that I mentioned in Chapter 3, but for present purposes it will not be necessary to use them. Remember that the best map for a job is not necessarily the most intricate.)

The modular view sees minitheories as consisting of two major parts, each of which has four subdivisions. The two parts are called HEAD and TALE. A summary of what these refer to is given in Figure 4.1. The HEAD contains the information that tells you what the module is *for*. It corresponds to the 'name' of a computer file, or the size and location of an island or an amoeba. (As you look at Figure 4.1, remember that the contents of the 'egg shape' show you everything that characterizes a minitheory; this is different from the images of the amoeba or the island, where the two-dimensional shape is supposed to suggest the domain of experience to which it applies – the part of the minitheory that I am now calling HEAD.) It gives a specification of the circumstances in which, and the purposes for which, that module – or rather the knowledge contained in its TALE – is to be used. HEAD is an acronym for the four ingredients of this specification.

Hub

First there is the hub, which describes the main kind of concept, event or scenario that the module is good for, what it is *about*. It specifies what is to be treated as the topic, the focus or the content. If an experienced pupil in a school has built up a set of minitheories for different teachers, then the hub of each tells her how to recognize them. An experienced teacher will have different modules in his mind that correspond to different teaching topics and units of work. The hub may consist of perceptual attributes, linguistic descriptions, or both. When we refer to a 'concept' we are talking about a hub.

Environment

The second part of the HEAD is the environment or context within which the module is believed to be effective. How to treat

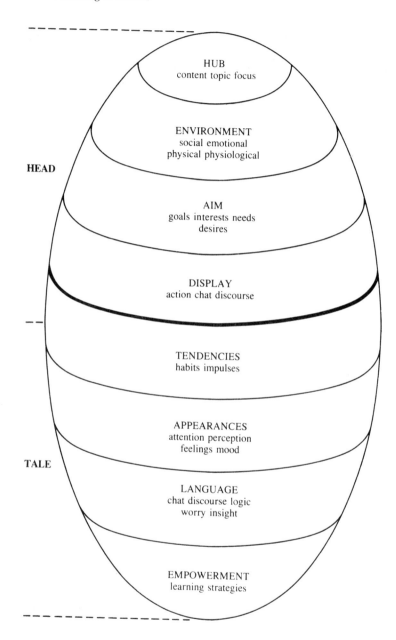

HUB
content topic focus

ENVIRONMENT
social emotional
physical physiological

AIM
goals interests needs
desires

DISPLAY
action chat discourse

TENDENCIES
habits impulses

APPEARANCES
attention perception
feelings mood

LANGUAGE
chat discourse logic
worry insight

EMPOWERMENT
learning strategies

HEAD

TALE

Figure 4.1. The constituents of a minitheory.

something may depend not only on what it is but on when and where it occurs. People's typical way of relating to their parents or their children, for example, is often dependent on who else happens to be around at the time – the *social* environment. Pupils may relate to teachers when they are out of school on a trip in a way that is very different from their normal demeanour in school.

These illustrations show the dependency of performance on social environment; but other features of the context in which people find themselves also have an effect on the kinds of skill that become available. *Emotion* and mood have powerful effects on the nature of cognition. When we are happy, happy memories are easy to find; but when we are sad or depressed, it is hard to recall 'the good times'. This effect has been demonstrated experimentally. People who were asked to learn a list of words when they were in a happy mood recalled the words better on a later occasion if they were happy again at the time. Similarly, and perhaps more surprisingly, things learnt in a sad mood were recalled better when the person was again sad.[2]

This might give us pause for thought if our aim as teachers is to create in the classroom as relaxed and co-operative an atmosphere as possible – knowing that, at the end of the year, our pupils will be required to retrieve what they know in conditions of competition and considerable stress. Most people are familiar with the experience of the mind 'going blank' when they are anxious, and this is due to the fact that the anxious circumstances do not match the environment specification that is part of the HEAD of the knowledge we want. Only slowly, as we sit staring glassy-eyed at the exam paper, does the burst of anxiety die down sufficiently for some of the relevant files to be found again. (The tidal wave receded, allowing our islands of knowledge to re-emerge.)

As well as the social and the emotional environment, the *physical* situation we are in also has a part to play. When people are asked to remember things in a different room from the one in which they learnt them, their performance is poorer.[3] Two British psychologists have even carried out the unlikely experiment of giving deep-sea divers a list of words to learn, either when they were on the beach or when they were submerged – and showed a large drop in their ability to recall them when they were tested in the alternative environment.[4]

In an equivalent test, another psychologist has shown that the *physiological* state of learners needs to be recreated at the time of recall if they are to do as well as they can. Two groups of undergraduates at Hull University were asked to learn a route on a map. One had previously had a drink of orange juice, and the other had had the juice with a strong draught of vodka in it. The next day they returned to the laboratory to be tested on their memory, whereupon half the previously 'sober' group were sober again and half were given the alcohol, and similarly for the previous 'drunk' group. The results showed that the two sub-groups which were in the same state on both occasions – that is, the sober–sober *and* the drunk–drunk groups – performed significantly better that the groups that had been switched. Of course, this works only within limits: too much vodka and it gets increasingly hard to learn the map at all![5] But such results make you wonder whether, if you have been revising late at night, full of instant coffee, it might not improve your success if you went into the examination hall in the same state. They certainly show why dress rehearsals are so important: if you suddenly switch from performing in jeans in a church hall with a cigarette in your hand to the full production with lights, costume, make-up and audience, without a bridge of simulation across which your performance can travel, you are asking for trouble.

Aim

The third element of the HEAD is the aim. Knowledge is indexed not only according to *what* it is (the hub) and *where and when* it is to be used (the environment), but also *why* you have it; what it is for. For something to be retrieved it needs to be appropriate to the external conditions, but it must also be relevant in terms of your needs, goals, interests, desires and purposes. In fact, the string that binds the bundle of a minitheory together is its function: if things that look different nevertheless turn out to be equivalent, in terms of their significance to you, then they are likely to be grouped together.[6]

So we may well find (as we shall see in Chapter 6) that pupils in school switch their attitude, learning style and even level of achievement with respect to the same subject or teacher when something shifts in their own matrix of internal priorities; and that pupils with different hopes and priorities respond quite differently to the 'same' situation, such as a good or bad teacher. A 'good' student *attends* to the 'good' teacher and *struggles* with the 'bad one; a 'bad' student *struggles* with the 'good' teacher and *mucks about* with the 'bad' one, to give a rather stereotyped illustration.

Display

The final part of the HEAD is the form of display which the person anticipates will be required in order to deal with the situation she faces. It contains a crude summary, more or less accurate, of the *kind* of performance that the TALE of its minitheory is capable of providing. Thus the knowledge base on which people draw may again be different, even though the 'topic' is the same, if the type of response that they are expecting changes. Some modules are specialized for producing spontaneous action – such as those used in skilled performances like playing a sport or musical instrument – and they may have little or no ability within them to explain how they are operating. Others may be good at producing informal styles of speech but lack the skills within them for translating fluent and persuasive chat into an academic argument. Others still may *only* generate scholarly discourse and be absolutely useless when it comes to getting around in the real world.

For example, a classic study of black American pupils showed that the form and complexity of the language that these young people used depended critically on the age, race and perceived trustworthiness of the person to whom they were talking.[7] If this person was black, friendly and informal, their language was much more fluent and intricate than if she or he was white and 'teacherly'. In the presence of 'teachers' these children anticipate, rightly or wrongly, that a certain, more formal, style of discourse is required, one which they are very unskilled at producing. But with friends, where the expectations of the appropriate 'voice' are quite different, fluent talk *about the same topics* can be readily produced.

The general idea of HEADs allows us to make sense of a common observation that is otherwise rather puzzling – the fact that people often display different attitudes and knowledge about the same topic in different contexts. Although the hub is the same, if the other parts of the HEAD – the environment, aim and expected display – are sufficiently different, then different TALEs, if they exist, will be brought into play. Thus from the outside it may look as if we are holding contradictory points of view about the 'same' topic, while from the inside we are actually responding from different minitheories that just happen to share the same name.

Sex for adolescents (and even perhaps for adults too) is such a topic. There is a rather clinical set of information that is inscribed somewhere on a file called 'Biology lessons'; a more lurid set of visual images that derive from surreptitious experiences with pornographic magazines or videos; an affected bravado that goes along with the showing-off and dirty jokes that are the stock in trade of many adolescent groups; and finally the panicky, tactile excitement of one's first 'real' experiences, which are about 95 per cent feeling and at most 5 per cent discussion. Each of these minitheories will be displayed at different times, in different contexts and each may embody attitudes that are at odds with the others.

Now let me briefly introduce the TALE, which is also an acronym, this time for remembering the kinds of thing that a minitheory can *do*. The TALE contains the capabilities that are made available to the person when that module is retrieved and activated.

Tendencies

First, we might single out the tendencies to act and respond which are stored. These are all the habits, dispositions and expectations that are associated with the minitheory. They are our ways of dealing, as skilfully as we know how, with whatever it is that we have decided we are faced with. Having diagnosed the present situation as being 'A French lesson with Mrs Dimmock', we are thereby set to respond in certain ways, to adopt certain attitudes and to expect certain things. When Mrs Dimmock shouts at someone, this constitutes a violation of the expected situation and

Figure 4.2. A hidden dalmatian.

results in a startled and attentive class (a very different situation from Mr Mandrake's class, where he shouts all the time and it has no effect at all). Our minitheory about our situation primes us to adopt a particular demeanour: the one that past experience has shown to work best.

Appearances

Secondly, the TALE contains information about appearances, and the direction of attention. Our 'common sense' tells us that we perceive things as they are and, having identified them, we respond; it supposes that all the work of perception comes before the identification. However, the work of the constructivists that we reviewed in Chapter 1 shows us that this is not so. What happens is that we look at the world and collect enough information from it to come up with an idea about what is 'out there' – that is, select a minitheory that might fit the situation. Having done so, the minitheory indicates what *also* ought to be present (if it is what you have hypothesized it to be), and your attention is then directed *by your hypothesis* to look out for, or even to create, those features which will act as confirmation.

Look at the pictures in Figures 4.2 and 4.3. Once you 'see' the

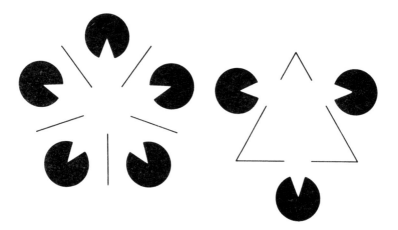

Figure 4.3. Two illusory shapes.

dog in the first picture, your mind will automatically fill in details, like the dog's hind leg, to confirm the perception, and will equally automatically decide what is important and what is irrelevant, what is 'salient' and what is mere background. Likewise in the second picture your mind has decided that the best way to make sense of each drawing is as a 'something' partially obscuring several 'something elses'. But in order to sustain this hypothesis it has to 'touch up' the scene in a few sneaky ways: it actually fills in shadowy (but quite visible) outlines for the 'top' shape; it gives you a sense that this shape is actually nearer to you than the background (as it would be if it were lying on top of the others); and it makes the shape itself appear somewhat whiter or brighter than the background – again as it would do if it were 'really' obscuring the rest of the scene.

These demonstrations are not merely 'party tricks'. They reveal in a very clear fashion something that is a general and constant feature of the way our minds work: that what we 'see' is not just a direct reflection of what is 'out there', but is a construction, based on our own accumulated history of interactions with the world. One way to put this is to say that we see things in terms of what we can do about them; perception is in part at least determined by the module through which we have chosen to look at the situation.

I want to include under 'appearances' the way that things seem to us emotionally as well as perceptually. When we perceive something, it very often comes with an associated feeling. We see something as a 'puppy' and feel warmly towards it. We hear a remark in the playground and feel scared. We notice a colleague in the staffroom and suddenly feel guilty as we remember something we have forgotten to do. These feelings are an important part of the appearance of things which is stirred into perception by the particular minitheory that has been selected. If I do not 'recognize' Mr Mandrake, I do not feel guilty. If I hear the remark as a joke, I feel amused rather than anxious. Emotions arise as the shadows of our interpretations of events; they are not inherent in the events themselves.

Language

The next part of the TALE is the part that lets it talk – the language part. As I noted above, some modules are very well equipped with ways of expressing their knowledge in words, while others are much more taciturn, concerning themselves with actions rather than commentaries. But even those that do contain verbal components are not all of the same kind. Language can be produced in many 'registers' – or 'voices', as they have been called.[8] Let me expand briefly on this point. Much *social* or *vernacular* language, such as that being used by the black American pupils in the research I quoted just now, is very situation-dependent: it presupposes a good deal of knowledge on the part of the person to whom you are talking, and much of the meaning is intentionally implicit. If we take a snatch of such language out of context, it may be quite uninterpretable. ('Well, he showed it to her and she goes – you know her – she goes, "That's *amazing*, but you'd better not let *her* get her greasy little mitts on it . . .".') In context, however, such speech is fluent, economical and often extremely evocative.

The main purpose of social language, and the knowledge that underpins it, is to get things done with people: to get thoughts shared, plans agreed, friendships tested or cemented, time pleasantly passed, grievances aired, and so on; and it is evaluated in these terms. The personalities and relationships of the people conversing are usually important to the discussion. The content of what is being talked about is usually (though not always) fairly obviously related to the purpose of the conversation. And this content is frequently an acceptable jumble of fact, opinion, belief, hearsay and conjecture. It often highlights what is bizarre, exciting or funny in terms of one's implicit, lay theories about the world, and can be completely disconnected from one's intellectual knowledge on the one hand, or one's own personal feelings and beliefs on the other.

However, there is another world of language entirely, which we might call *lesson* language, where things are quite different. In situations where you cannot or may not presume shared knowledge, or where the tone of discussion is set by special rules and customs, you need to be able to switch into a different register, one that often uses longer words, more complex sentence structure and different intonations. You are required by these conventions to be explicit, to be prepared to offer rational justification for whatever you assert, and to distinguish clearly between matters of fact, speculation, judgement and personal opinion. Personalities are supposed to be unimportant in this form of discourse (though they are often very relevant in fact, as people try to impress imagined examiners or prespective employers). And the content of a discussion may be quite unrelated to the reasons why the contributors have come together: it does not arise 'organically', so to speak, out of the personalities and their priorities, but from some preformed agenda.

Some people have developed minitheories that incorporate the linguistic styles of the different social groups to which they belong. They may be able to talk as fluently (though using quite different voices) to their children's teachers, or their family doctor, as they do to their children and their friends. And a voice may lie low, tucked up in its own minitheory, even for long periods, if that minitheory goes unused for a while. For example, it is sometimes disconcerting to be in the middle of an energetic reunion with old friends and to realize that you have 'regressed', in terms of style of conversation, sense of humour and so on, to being a person that you had quite forgotten – and whose attitudes may be rather out of line with those of the person you now believe yourself to be.

It follows that files that are designed to produce language of predominantly one kind or the other will be 'formatted' in quite different ways. A school file such as the one used for storing 'science' must be tidy, well organized, capable of being accessed readily and flexibly, and based, where possible, on 'first principles'. A social file, on the other hand, can be quite unsystematic and set up to highlight little trinkets of information which happen to be bizarre, exciting or funny, rather than 'key points' and 'definitions'. One of the problems that faces school pupils is the need to learn the new kind of format that is required for each new 'subject' they meet. The tendency to try to collect 'intellectual' forms of knowledge on a file that has already been formatted for 'social' use creates serious problems, as we shall see in Chapter 6.

One especially important component of the language compartment is the language we used to talk to ourselves: the language of thought. Again there are several sorts, of which we might note just three here. There is the language of *intellectual thought*, of rational enquiry and figuring things out. There is the language of *worry*, which is a much less rational pursuit of trains of thought that bring to life our fears, and which serve more as warrants for those fears than potential solutions of them. And there is the language of *insight*, which bubbles up from tacit sources and seems to represent to the conscious mind something that had previously been known or understood at the inarticulate level of tendencies and appearances. Note that I am including here not just the contents of thought, but the skills, patterns or styles of thought that go along with the contents. As with the overt use of language, a minitheory determines the way that thought occurs, as well as what there is to think about.

Empowerment

The final ingredient, the 'tip' of the TALE, is empowerment, by which I mean any learning amplifiers or strategies that are associated with a minitheory. We shall consider learning strategies in more detail in Chapter 6.

SUMMARY AND READING

In this chapter we have reviewed a number of ways of looking at the 'modular mind': as islands emerging from the sea of experience; as amoebae gradually conforming to the shape of the domains of experience to which they apply; and as computer files, each developed to do a particular kind of job. As a way of remembering the different ingredients, both of the contents of a file and of its 'heading' or 'index entry', we used the idea of HEADs and TALEs. HEADs comprises a hub (what the file is about), an environment (containing social, emotional, physical and physiological features), an aim (the purpose the file is good for) and a display (the kind of performance it will produce). TALEs contain information that determines tendencies (habits, impulses, dispositions), appearances (perception, attention, feeling), language (of different sorts) and empowerment (learning strategies that will help to solve problems in that domain).

A popular exposition of the modular point of view, though one that is more coarse-grained than mine, is Robert Ornstein's *Multimind*. Better, but more technical, is Marvin Minsky's *The*

Society of Mind. Close to the present view is that of Roger Schank, developed in the course of several books, most recently *Explanation Patterns.* The major issues that concern the best way to represent the structure of our knowledge are reviewed in *Issues in Cognitive Modeling,* edited by A. M. Aitkenhead and J. M. Slack, and by Philip Johnson-Laird in *The Computer and the Mind.* The controversy between Zajonc and Lazarus about whether cognition precedes or follows emotion (which seems to me to reduce to the ambiguity between 'tacit mental process' and 'conscious mental product' contained in the word 'cognitive') is reviewed by Nico Frijda.[9]

NOTES

(1)   Samuel Butler, *Notebooks.*

(2)   Bower, G. H. (1981) Mood and memory. *American Psychologist*, **36**, 129-48.

(3)   Smith, S. M., Glenberg, A. M. and Bjork, R. A. (1978) Environmental context and human memory. *Memory and Cognition*, **6**, 342–53.

(4)   Godden, D. R. and Baddeley, A. D. (1975) Context-dependent memory in two natural environments: on land and underwater. *British Journal of Psychology*, **66**, 325–31.

(5)   Lowe, G. (1980) State-dependent recall decrements with moderate doses of alcohol. *Current Psychological Research*, **1**, 3–8.

(6)   Concepts have to be defined functionally: there are an infinite number of ways of breaking up the world on the basis of perception alone. The point was made long ago by Bruner, J. S., Goodnow, J. J. and Austin, G. A. (1956) *A Study of Thinking.* New York: Wiley.

(7)   Labov, W. (1973) The logic of non-standard English. In Keddie, N. (ed.), *Tinker, Tailor . . . the Myth of Cultural Deprivation.* Harmondsworth: Penguin.

(8)   Scholes, R. and Kellogg, R. (1966) *The Nature of Narrative.* New York: Oxford University Press.

(9)   Ornstein, R. (1986) *Multimind.* London: Macmillan. Minsky, M. (1988) *The Society of Mind.* London: Pan. Schank, R. C. (1986) *Explanation Patterns.* Hillsdale, NJ: Erlbaum. Aitkenhead, A. M. and Slack, J. M. (eds) (1985) *Issues in Cognitive Modeling.* London: Erlbaum. Johnson-Laird, P. N. (1988) *The Computer and the Mind.* London: Fontana. Frijda, N. H. (1986) *The Emotions.* Cambridge: Cambridge University Press.

Chapter 5

Simple Learning

Assume that we have deliberately made it our task to live in this unknown world of ours; to adjust ourselves to it as well as we can; to take advantage of the opportunities we can find in it; and to explain it, if possible. . . . If we have made this our task, there is no more rational procedure than the method of trial and error – of conjecture and refutation.

Karl Popper[1]

Now I wish to explore a little further the learning options inherent in the minitheory view. Let us start with the simple case of *editing the TALE*. Typically, an event occurs which seems to lie within, or close to, an island of competence; the 'analogy' is made that this new thing is another example of the class of things that the minitheory knows how to deal with; expectations are set in place as to how it behaves and how it will respond to various kinds of interaction; habits are put in motion – and an unexpected result occurs. 'I thought she looked like a possible friend, so I offered her one of my sweets – and she ran off with the packet.' 'I thought Mr Mandrake had it in for me, so I kept out of his way – and then I got a glowing report from him at the end of term.' 'I specially invited my tutor in to watch me teach my best class – and the little devils ran amok on me.' 'I thought I really knew *Twelfth Night*, but the mock GCSEs asked all kinds of questions that I didn't know how to answer.' The most obvious response in all these cases is to make a modification or an addition to the relevant 'body of knowledge', so that I shall be better prepared next time.

This fundamental, continuous, spontaneous process of checking and adjusting is our natural learning ability. We were born with it, as were all the higher animals, and without it babies could not even begin to learn to manipulate their mothers, nor mothers their babies. It is a relatively slow but very reliable process of tuning, just as one fine-tunes a radio to get the station as clear as possible – and if it is faint, keeps listening with half an ear for the need to retune from time to time. This gradual experimentation and refinement is the unsung hero of learning, being for the most part tacit and inconspicuous. Yet it accounts for the vast majority of our early learning and continues to function throughout life as we meet new people, live in new houses, drive new cars and visit new places for our holidays. There is a Japanese proverb which says, 'Don't learn it; get used to it'. Tuning is our ability to get used to things and to find ever more effective ways of rubbing along with them.

Look at it in terms of the amoeba image. Suppose you could look inside someone's head, say an 8-year-old's, and see one small area of her mind laid out as in Figure 5.1. Four minitheories are lying fairly close together, as they all relate to scenarios in which a significant feature is the lowering of something 'solid' into or on to something 'squishy'. The *bed* script refers to the whole bedtime ritual, including the feeling of getting into a nice soft bed. The *boat* scenario relates to trips to the local park to sail a toy yacht on the pond. *Drink* contains general information about what drinks she likes, what they taste like, when it is usual to take one drink rather than another ('Ovaltine for *breakfast*?'), and what happens when you drop a sugar cube into a cup of tea (or a glass of cola). The *bath* minitheory records expectations about the bathtime rituals, including what happens when she gets into the water.

Now suppose that our 8-year-old finds herself in her classroom one day confronted by a teacher who has decided it is time for his pupils to do some science. He has borrowed a 'measuring cylinder' and a cylindrical copper block that just fits it from a friend who teaches secondary science. He fills the glass container half full of water and then asks the assembled children, 'What do you think will happen to the water level if I put the block into the tube?' Our hypothetical pupil has never seen this scientific equipment before, so she has no ready-made memory on which to draw.

She can, however, use one of her four minitheories as an analogy. If this new situation is like jumping on the bed – in the

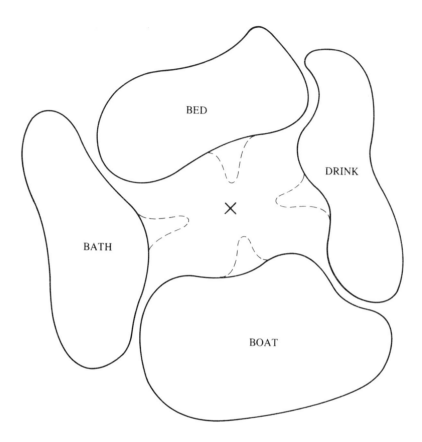

Figure 5.1. Minitheories extending themselves to cope with a 'problem'.

analogy her solid body is the block and the soft bed is the water –
then the water level should go down, as it is 'squashed' by the
weight. If it is like launching her (metal) boat on the pond, then,
on the basis of her experience, nothing will happen to the water
level. Neither will it if she draws an unconscious parallel between
block and water and the situation of dropping a sugar lump into a
cup of tea: to the naked eye the level of the tea in the cup is not
affected. Finally, if she chooses the analogy of herself getting into
the bath, she may draw on the experience of being intrigued by the
fact that the water in the bath goes up, and she may even be able to
justify her answer to the teacher (on the basis of a conversation

with her father) by saying that the block will 'push the water out of the way'.

In each case she is making a sensible attempt to extend what she already knows to cover the new event. And it is a matter of particular experiences – even luck, we might say – whether she just happens to select the analogy that delivers the 'right' answer. Notice too that her ability to rationalize her intuition depends on whether the selected analogy makes available an explanation. The absence of justification certainly does not mean that she 'didn't think' or 'isn't very bright'. For her, as for adults much of the time, the minitheory that she is using to get something done does not at the same time provide a commentary or account of how or why she is acting or responding as she is.

Whatever her answer, she will learn something from the experience. If the amoebic advance proves 'successful', its boundary is redrawn to include the new type of event. If it is not, then the boundary in that region is withdrawn and sharpened – to prevent a similar overgeneralization in the future. In addition, the content of the minitheories – their TALEs – may also be updated. Depending on how the TALE was constructed in the first place, it is possible to modify any or all of its constituents. If what went wrong was a physical action, then it is likely that what needs tuning is the sense of tendencies and appearances. To revert to our earlier examples: rather than set out to beat the little thief to a pulp (or maybe as well as doing that) the young child who had his sweets pinched may spend time scrutinizing her from a distance, trying to find something about her that looks different, which can be used as a future aid to deciding who to share his treats with. At the same time his generosity may be generally withdrawn, while he attempts to find a satisfactory way of redrawing the internal boundaries. The adolescent tries a more-cheery-than-usual 'Morning, sir' to Mr Mandrake at the beginning of the following term – as a tentative experiment, to see what sort of reply he gets. Again, intuitive adjustments are made and checked out, which rely either on drawing slightly different perceptual distinctions, or on modifying habits, or, more usually, on both.

The other ways of modifying the TALE are through language and the development of new learning strategies – empowerment. We shall leave these till Chapter 6 and turn now to the other main form of learning minitheories can undergo: editing the HEAD.

DISEMBEDDING AND THE TRANSFER PROBLEM

Most existing approaches to learning have focused on the acquisition of new knowledge and skill – on editing our mental TALEs. This emphasis has been apparent in both formal and intuitive theories of learning, and in preschool, primary and secondary sectors of the education business. Of course, this kind of learning is important. But the minitheory perspective brings into the limelight a whole other sphere of learning: the ways in which the HEADs of what we know are altered by experience, so that we come to maximize the potential of the knowledge and capability that we already possess. Pupils in school have to realize (in both senses: 'converting into usable form' as well as 'becoming aware of') the many ways in which things they have picked up in one set of conditions are also useful in *other* settings. Student teachers have to learn the limits of applicability of their intuitive theories of teaching, and also the actual relevance of other capabilities – dealing with emotionally laden conflict, for example – that may be written on files that at first sight seem to have little to do with the formalized, professional world of a school.

In this process of gradually reappraising the relevance of what we know, we can discern a developmental drift away from the close attachment of what we learnt to its initial learning context and towards greater generalizability and 'abstraction'. Not only do the *particular* features of the HEADs change; there is a progressive stripping away of the rich but incidental details of the learning contexts, leaving more clear-cut descriptions of the particular 'concepts' and purposes with which the TALE is capable of dealing. To start with, every element of the HEAD is potentially relevant: the room, feeling and the company *could* all be as important, as indicators of when to whine and when to shut up, as the presence of mother and hunger. The indicative and the accidental are bundled up together in experience, and it is only as a result of much additional experimentation and interaction that it becomes clear which is which.

It is now time to bring in another of the main themes that I trailed a little earlier: the assumed pre-eminence of intellectual forms and cognitive aspects of learning. The focus of schooling is mainly, even now, on the skills of reading or calculating or evaluating evidence or holding rational discussions. Even in the 'practical' subjects you have to be able to describe, explain and evaluate, as well as 'merely' to do. From this point of view the classroom is essentially cognitive and incidentally social and emotional. From the pupils' point of view, however, the priorities are reversed – and the younger they are, in general, the more so. For the teacher what he is trying to teach is 'figure' and the rest is 'ground'; for the young child the personalities, relationships and feelings are at the centre of her world, and cognitive activity – in the sense of learning about *things* and *ideas* – receives attention, and proceeds well, only when the socioemotional pressures are weak enough to fade, temporarily, from the limelight of her consciousness.[2]

Because children's awareness is predominantly social, the HEADs of what they learn are crammed with social detail, some of which is truly predictive of how to behave, and much of which it will be in their best interests to moult, as they grow older, so that their cognitive learning comes to have more power and scope. It is this process that Margaret Donaldson and others have called 'disembedding'.[3] Children's cognition, all their skills of understanding and interacting with the world around them, is initially embedded within surrounding layers of contextual detail, referring to the concrete personal circumstances of their own lives and needs. As development proceeds, so wider experience gradually dissolves these layers away, like the slow sucking of a gobstopper, leaving a more and more evident, more and more deployable, kernel of concept and process (see Figure 5.2).

Wherever learners may be in the course of their refining and disembedding, they can be confronted with problems that vary enormously in terms of the problems' relationship to their experience and interests. And this relationship will determine how the problem is tackled, and how successfully. For instance, what we might call *spontaneously embedded* problems are those that arise naturally in the course of people's on-going, self-chosen, often social activities. Here learning is 'wholly embedded in a context of action, direct perception, purpose and feeling' (this and the subsequent quotations are from Margaret Donaldson[4]). A minitheory is already running which makes available ways of handling the situation, resources for investigating it, and sensible questions to ask about it. The E for empowerment in the TALE make available learning strategies that enable you to grapple with

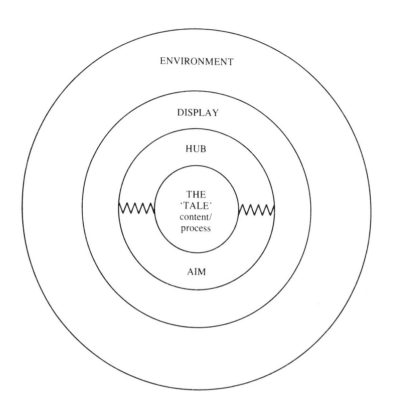

Figure 5.2. The developmental gobstopper.

problems that seem meaningful and interesting.

Then there are *life-world embedded* problems, in which 'thinking arises directly from one's own life concerns, even though it is not about the immediate present'. It may involve 'extensions into the past and the future, but still the focus is on the personal life – plans, memories, hopes and fears'. Even though the problem is raised by someone else (usually, in school, a teacher) and involves a redirection of the flow of thought and perception, nevertheless minitheories can be brought into play within which the problem looks tractable, sensible and engaging.

Further down the scale there are *conceptually embedded* problems, which we might divide into the *linguistically* and the *symbolically* embedded. In both we require 'thinking which is called for by a problem set by someone else . . . unconnected with anything we have been doing, or are planning to do, or that spontaneously engages our minds'. To tackle such problems requires 'the ability to think and talk about things that are not only further off in space and time (or entirely hypothetical) but remote from the thrust of one's own concerns'. To do that, a person needs a knowledge system that is fairly well advanced in the direction of internal disembedding; where much of the contextual specificity of the minitheories has been worn away, leaving a relatively abstract set of concept/process packages that are internally linked together (see below). This allows a form of thought that is developmentally quite late, and that approximates to Piaget's 'formal operations' – though in the present model this ability is seen to arise in an evolutionary, and not a revolutionary, fashion.

In a linguistically embedded problem, the words and terms are meaningful, even though they do not, taken together, point to a pre-existing domain of familiarity. With such a problem you have to take a 'long shot' as to what it might relate to, as you search around for a minitheory that might be ransacked or doctored to come up with some ideas. As Donaldson reminds us, this is a risky business which can easily go awry:

> The meaningful words may merely tempt us, rousing in us the old familiar sense-making urge . . . by means of which we contrive to slot the problem into some setting with which we are familiar, in which we feel we know the rules. If the setting that we provide is appropriate to the problem, then all goes well. But if the setting is inappropriate – and especially if, without noticing, we alter the problem slightly to fit – then at once we are in trouble.

A symbolically embedded problem is for young learners the most remote of all from first-hand, unmediated experience. (Professional scientists, engineers and so on may have come to re-embed their symbolic knowledge within appropriate domains of technical experience with which their training and careers have provided them.) With such a problem the pupil has nothing in her mind that can mislead her – but neither does she have any pre-existing resources on which to draw. To cope well with these, she must have already developed learning strategies of considerable abstraction.

DISEMBEDDING AND SCHOOL

This analysis has two important implications for the organization of schooling. First, it means that, while development is allowed to proceed at some 'natural' rate along a gradually broadening continuum of experience, so this process of disembedding can track along with it.[5] As children find themselves in new situations that form an endless range of variations on familiar themes, so this distinguishing of relevant from irrelevant details becomes more precise. New forms of cognitive organization evolve out of earlier ones, in the way that one word can be turned into a succession of others by changing one letter at a time. This issue of *pacing* therefore becomes very important if one of our goals as educators is to 'teach for transfer'.

Such jumps or discontinuities as there are need to be kept small if the evolutionary process is to continue successfully. When stepping stones are close enough together, you can cross the stream using the familiar strategies of walking and hopping. But put them too far apart and either evolution is arrested or an entirely new way of proceeding – swimming or renting a boat – has to be used instead. These are the learning strategies that enable people to overcome larger obstacles to learning, and to undertake bigger challenges, than the natural learning ability itself could cope with. The younger the child, again, the less likely are these more sophisticated strategies to have been developed, and the more likely therefore is learning to face an interruption and a discontinuity. Such is the situation that confronts many pupils in the course of their educational career, in the physical transition from home to school, from one stage of schooling to another, or in the mental jump from one topic to another.

The second implication is that, if we want people to be able to use a certain minitheory in a particular type of situation, one which can be foreseen, we need to ensure that *all* the conditions are conducive to its retrieval. Relevance is not a property of knowledge that can be magically intuited, even by the 'bright'; and the sense of relevance is holistic. We not only have to present a familiar kind of problem, but we have to make sure that all the elements of the environment that people are working in – social, emotional, physical and physiological – are similar to those that attended the original learning experiences. If we do not want our pupils' knowledge to be so closely tied to particular situations, then we have to pay attention to the process of *disembedding* knowledge from its original context in our teaching. We have a choice.

GETTING STARTED ON MATHS: A CASE STUDY

We might illustrate several of the key ideas of this chapter with another case study: the problems that face the young child in the area of mathematics learning.[6] During the second, third and fourth years of life, she will have picked up a variable amount of skill in the areas of number and sums that is embedded in a wide variety of different minitheories. She will have discovered that numbers can be attributes or names of things. 'I am 3. My big sister is 9.' 'We live at Number 17.' 'Our car is a 316.' And these are muddled up with all kinds of other, apparently equivalent, labels and features. 'I am Susan.' 'My sister is Tami.' 'Our house is a bungalow.' 'Our car is grey.' These are different from numbers that describe a characteristic *group* of things. 'There are six of us in our family.' 'I've got three bricks.' 'Socks come in pairs.' 'I want three fish fingers.'

There are numbers that involve counting and sequencing, such as games that involve counting the number of traffic lights as we go along in the car, or counting the stairs up to the bathroom in Granny's house. There are numbers that give instructions on what to do, as the dice in Snakes and Ladders tells her how many squares to move. There are numbers to do with time and waiting: the flashing lights on the video machine seem to be connected with time; her bedtime is supposed to be 6.30; she sometimes has to wait five (interminable) minutes for something to happen. There are visual numbers on the boxes and bottles that come from the shops that are to do with how much they cost. There are simple sums that involve saying how many fish fingers she has had if she decides she wants an extra one, or how many knives and forks need to be put out when Granny and Grandpa come for tea. And so on and so on.

Some children, by the time they start in primary school, will be quite adept with simple sums involving small numbers, and will even have begun to tie all the different uses of number together and to see that there is something in common. Most will have lots of fragments, such as I have illustrated, embedded within a host of minitheories that are not themselves *about* number, but that contain situation-specific, idiosyncratic references to numbers and sums. Such children, the majority, have no concept of number as such – in just the same way as they have no notion of colour as such or motion as such, yet are perfectly able to use colour words and movement words in particular, familiar scenarios. Thus, as Martin Hughes has shown, they can happily tell you that there are three beans in a tin if there were two before and you added one. But they get cross and fretful if you try and get them to say 'what two and one make'.[7] Little pieces of number knowledge are scattered across a vast range of scripts, the main function of which is not to do sums, but to interact harmoniously with important other people. The cognitive operations (and their success) are subordinated to more pressing social and emotional purposes. In fact, you can often have *more* fun getting it wrong, and being deliberately (or inadvertently) silly, than by being correct.

Now put your child in school and see whether she is given the stepping stones that enable her to move from this useful, higgledy-piggledy mess of number-fragments, in an evolutionary progression, to a tidy, disembedded, portable minitheory of numbers and arithmetical operations as such. Frequently teachers' impatience and anxiety about numeracy (and the same argument applies even more strongly to literacy) lead them to behave with increasing disregard for children's real, inevitable difficulties, and to turn a process that needed gentle persuasion and judicious support into a nightmare and an impossibility. With sighs of disappointment, they may narrow their attention to a diminishing proportion of their pupils, as more and more of their classmates, showing signs of developing 'special educational needs', lag behind and drop out of earshot. What are you to do when someone is calling to you from the other bank with increasing exasperation, but you can neither see the stepping stones nor swim?

Even if she *has* arrived at school with number-fragments that were well enough developed to provide the foundations for some guided disembedding, she may not be able to retrieve them because her total environment is changed so comprehensively. Of course the physical surroundings are different. Of course there are now a lot more small people around. Of course the teacher is not her mother. But also the aim is different: now she is trying to be *better* than the others or not to fail. The mode of display and discourse is different: it is all bound up with writing, and with learning a confusing vocabulary of technical words like 'times', 'difference', 'makes', 'goes into', 'take away' – which *look* familiar but which seem to bear no relationship to their everyday counterparts. Association to clocks, fabrication and Chinese meals do not seem to help. After several experiences of being told that the 'difference' between 11 and 6 is *not* that 11 has two numbers and 6 has only one, nor that 11 is pointy while 6 is curly (as happened to Martin Hughes' daughter), it is not surprising that some children give up looking for existing minitheories to use as analogical stepping stones, and crouch down in the long grass on their side of the cognitive divide until the teacher gives up shouting at them and turns away.

The process of disembedding can be accelerated by school, just as the growth of a plant can be hastened by judicious weeding and fertilizing, or the responsiveness of a horse be developed by suitable training. Cross-cultural research shows that one of the effects of formal schooling is to increase the abstractness and transferability of knowledge.[8] But when the pace of learning is set at a greater rate than the current learning strategies and capabilities of the learner can support, then there is a change inside the learner from involvement to defensiveness, and this, as we shall see in Chapter 7, can have long-term consequences that are deleterious to learning ability.

LINKING UP: LANGUAGE AND THOUGHT

One way in which mental organization changes, especially in the early years of life, is in the gradual refinement of the internal landscape of minitheories: they become more effective, more elegant, more comprehensive and more appropriate. But there is a second progression, which involves the linking up of originally separate minitheories. Although the basic layout of cognition is modular, with mental processes bundled up with descriptions of the situations in which and the tasks for which they are to be used, some of them nevertheless come to be able to talk to each other internally. This very useful trick requires both the kind of disembedding that we have just been talking about, and language. Daniel Dennett has proposed how this might have happened evolutionarily; it is very likely that an exactly parallel process happens in the development of the individual. Let me quote what Dennett calls his 'Just So Story'.

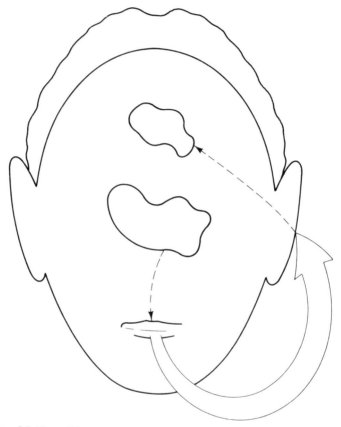

Figure 5.3. How talking to yourself can enable separate minitheories to get in touch with each other.

Imagine a community of creatures, our evolutionary ancestors, who have developed to the point where they (1) have a language, and (2) have discovered the survival advantages (for both species and individual) of co-operation, so that (3) they sometimes 'ask for help' and sometimes get it.

Then, one fine day, an 'unintended' short-circuit effect of this new social institution was 'noticed' by a creature. It 'asked' for help in an inappropriate circumstance, where there was no helpful audience to hear the request and respond. Except itself! When the creature heard its own request, the stimulation provoked just the sort of other-helping utterance production that the request from another would have caused. And to the creature's 'delight' it found that it had just provoked itself into answering its own question!

How could the activity of asking oneself questions be any less systematically futile than the activity of paying oneself a tip for making oneself a drink? All one needs to suppose is that there is some compartmentalization and imperfect *internal* communication between components of a creature's cognitive system [i.e. minitheories], so that one component can need the output of another component but be unable to address that component directly. Suppose the only way of getting component A to do its job is to provoke it into action by a sort of stimulus that normally comes from the outside, from another creature. If one day one discovers that one can play the role of this other and achieve a good result by autostimulation, the practice will blaze a valuable new communicative trail between one's internal components, a trail that happens to wander out into the public space of airwaves and acoustics. . ..

So in this Just So Story, the creatures got into the habit of talking [aloud] to themselves. And they found that it often had good results – often enough, in fact, to reinforce the practice. And they got better and better at it. In particular, they discovered an efficient shortcut: *sotto voce* talking to oneself, which later led to entirely silent talking to oneself. The silent process maintained the loop of self-stimulation but jettisoned the peripheral vocalisation [which] had the further benefit, opportunistically endorsed, of achieving a certain privacy. . ..[9]

This is an appealing way of showing how thought arises, in the life of the individual, as well as the species, as a means of overcoming the limitations of a mind that is constructed on essentially modular lines. Each file is well specialized for a particular range of jobs, and, being specialized it comes to solve the problems in its domain easily and elegantly. But this form of organization is not so good at coping when life becomes less routine and a much greater degree of disembedding is required. Language and thought, acting in the way Dennett has described, serve to increase enormously the power and the flexibility of the mind. By labelling minitheories with words we are able to dissect familiar scenarios into their stable ingredients, and thus, by bringing together these components in our minds, to explore ways of tackling situations which we have never yet experienced: a very useful learning ability indeed.

SUMMARY AND READING

Four broad kinds of learning were identified. The most familiar is editing the TALE – the content of a minitheory – to add to the store of knowledge and skill. Then there is refining the HEAD, especially the kind of refinement that discovers and eliminates features that are actually inessential to the scope of the minitheory – disembedding. Disembedding is a developmental process that requires certain conditions of pacing, in particular, to occur smoothly, and schooling needs to be aware of these. Next came the process whereby originally separate minitheories could be functionally linked together through the development of language and thought. Apart from the value of language in allowing external communication, it vastly increases the ability of different minitheories to refer to each other internally, and thus sows the seeds of creativity. Finally, we referred several times to the use and the growth of learning amplifiers, or learning strategies, which are special 'programs' that assist learning. It is to these that we turn our full attention in the next chapter.

An introduction to the kinds of learning discussed in this chapter is provided by David Rumelhart and Donald Norman in a book chapter, 'Accretion, tuning and restructuring'. Similar themes are explored in my earlier *Live and Learn: An Introduction to the Psychology of Growth and Change in Everyday Life*, especially chapters 4 and 5. The whole issue of embedding and disembedding, and its relevance to education, is explored in Margaret Donaldson's classic *Children's Minds*, and the special importance of the social context is demonstrated in her contribution, and several of the others, to *Making Sense*, edited by Jerome Bruner and Helen Haste. An earlier collection, *Social Cognition*, edited by George Butterworth and Paul Light, explores the research basis in more detail. The vexed question of how 'general-purpose' mental skills can be is well discussed in an article by David Perkins and Gavriel Salomon called 'Are cognitive skills context-bound?'.[10]

NOTES

(1) Karl Popper (1963) *Conjectures and Refutations*. London: Routledge & Kegan Paul.

(2) For a summary of some contributions to this growing study of 'social cognition', see Bruner, J. and Haste, H. (eds) (1987) *Making Sense: The Child's Construction of the World*. London: Methuen.

(3) Donaldson, M. (1978) *Children's Minds*. London: Fontana.

(4) Donaldson, M. (1987) The origins of inference. In Bruner and Haste (eds), *Making Sense*, op. cit.

(5) I am borrowing the notion of a developmental 'continuum' deliberately from Liedloff, J. (1986) *The Continuum Concept*. Harmondsworth: Penguin. She makes the similar (though I think more contentious) argument that a period of being literally a babe-in-arms is a necessary developmental stepping stone of which we deprive infants at our, and their, peril.

(6) The ideas in this section owe much to conversations with members of the Science and Mathematics Education Research Centre, University of Waikato, Hamilton, New Zealand, especially Margaret Carr, Jane McChesney and Jennifer Young-Loveridge.

(7) Hughes, M. (1986) *Children and Number: Difficulties in Learning Mathematics*. London: Fontana.

(8) Scribner, S. and Cole, M. (1973) Cognitive consequences of formal and informal education, *Science*, **182**, 553–9.

(9) Dennett, D. (1984) *Elbow Room: The Varieties of Free Will Worth Wanting*. Oxford: Clarendon Press.

(10) Rumelhart, D. and Norman, D. A. (1978) Accretion, tuning and restructuring: three modes of learning. In Cotton, J. W. and Klatzky, R. L. (eds), *Semantic Factors in Cognition*. Hillsdale, NJ: Erlbaum. Claxton, G. L. (1984) *Live and Learn: An Introduction to the Psychology of Growth and Change in Everyday Life*. London: Harper & Row; reissued (1988) Milton Keynes: Open University Press. Donaldson, *Children's Minds*, op. cit. Bruner and Haste (eds), *Making Sense*, op. cit. Butterworth, G. and Light, P. (eds) (1982) *Social Cognition*. Brighton: Harvester. Perkins, D. N. and Salomon, G. (1988) Are cognitive skills context-bound? *Educational Researcher*, **18**, 16–25.

Chapter 6

Learning Strategies

All our lives long, every day and every hour, we are engaged in the process of accommodating our changed and unchanged selves to changed and unchanged surroundings; living, in fact, is nothing else than this accommodation: when we fail in it a little we are stupid, when we fail flagrantly we are mad, when we suspend it temporarily we sleep, when we give up the attempt altogether we die.

Samuel Butler[1]

The natural learning ability which we introduced in the last chapter enables all learners, of whatever age, to modify and tune what they know in the light of experience. But it can only work slowly outwards from what is already known, and must therefore be restricted to experiences that are construed as being minor variations on existing themes. When something happens that does not fall within the 'coastal waters' of an established minitheory, therefore, one of three things must happen: the event is ignored; or it is distorted (as Margaret Donaldson described in the previous chapter) to fit into an existing template, so that answers of a kind become available, but they do not really fit the nature of the event; or other learning processes have to be used that are better able to deal with high degrees of disembeddedness and unfamiliarity. It is the third option that I want to explore in this chapter.

What we are talking about is a special breed of minitheories which are developed in order to deal explicitly with different kinds of strangeness – an unusual bodily feeling; some difficult chemistry homework; a surprising interaction with another child; getting lost on the way home from the shops. In terms of our HEADs and

TALEs, such a minitheory might look like this:

H = a kind of unusual occurrence
E = presence of someone to ask for help; to imitate
A = solving the problem; understanding what is happening
D = physical action; verbal explanation

T = experimenting; probing; imitating; etc.
A = paying attention; scrutinizing; eavesdropping; etc.
L = asking questions; figuring it out
E = 'what it all adds up to'

SPAWNING

As young children gain more and more experience, so their stock of minitheories becomes greater. Usually with the collaboration of another person – parent, sibling, friend or teacher – the minitheory that deals with a particular scenario becomes richer and more differentiated. Variations keep cropping up, either accidentally or deliberately contrived, which add more detail and flexibility to the child's way of responding in that area. And as this process of modifying, elaborating and enriching continues, so the minitheory comes to contain sub-skills for coping with particular kinds of contingency. An early example would be the way that the 'scripts' for feeding or nappy changing are gradually elaborated to contain a variety of games and playful interactions.

One subset of these might be imitation games, where the young child learns that a close sense of 'attunement' can be achieved by joining in the game of mimicking gestures and sounds that someone else is making.[2] Slowly the ability to imitate, and to use imitation as a way of promoting desirable forms of interaction, grows within other scripts, much as a baby grows within the body of its mother. Particularly if the same set of sub-skills has been maturing inside a number of *different* mental 'wombs' – if imitation has been developing within the minitheories for 'feeding', 'nappy changing', 'playing with Daddy' and so on – then there comes a point where this more general-purpose, transsituational ability is 'born', separated out from its originating context and constituted as a minitheory in its own right, with a HEAD that now refers not to the details of a particular, familiar interaction, but to a *style* of interaction that may deliver a sense of happy engagement with other people, even those who may be strangers, and even when the 'scenario' in which the child finds herself is an unfamiliar one.

The process I have just illustrated is, if you like, a variant of the shift towards disembedding that we discussed in Chapter 5. But instead of a whole minitheory gradually broadening its sphere of influence, a part which is seen to have a usefulness across a range of familiar situations can become dissected out, and begin to have a cognitive life of its own. Disembedding happens by the 'spawning' of sub-skills that have been found to have a 'range of convenience', as George Kelly called it,[3] well beyond the bounds of their parent scenarios.

This then is another powerful way in which the particular can grow towards the more general. Skills are never found without some sense of their applicability. But their HEADs can be remodelled to incorporate only the most crucial features that will predict their success, and to leave out everything that is in fact incidental.

At some point in the process of differentiation, experience may reveal not only new environments for an ability but new aims or purposes as well. One of the most important latent functions of an ability may be its power as a *learning strategy*. A set of tendencies that were originally developed in the context, and for the purpose, of having fun, may subsequently be discovered to have potential as a way of enhancing learning. Take imitation as an example again. At first its aim is the consolidation of social attunement – it provides a way for the child to feel in touch with those around him. But at some point a child may experiment with imitating his elder sister not when she is playing with him, but when she is engaged, in his presence, on some task of her own. What he discovers is that (sometimes) when he tries to do what she is doing, he gets the same result for himself. Now suppose that both he and his sister are simultaneously intent on solving similar problems: by watching and reproducing what *she* is doing, he may end up with the result that *he* wants. He wants to turn the TV on: do what she does. He wants to make Daddy laugh: see how Tami does it. Of course, the results will not be reliable. But he now has the bones of a very powerful 'learning amplifier', a strategy which will at least give him some hints as to how to proceed in situations where his own store of minitheories is not yet developed enough, or generalized enough, to provide an answer.

Remember that the last part of the TALE of a minitheory, its store of capability for self-empowerment, refers to the ideas it possesses about how to solve problems and deal with uncertainties that crop up in the domain. When I want a cuddle and nobody is present, what do I do? When I am in the middle of feeding and a choice piece of food drops on the floor, what do I do? Through experiences of successful problem-solving within the domain, the minitheory comes to accumulate its own tool-kit for fixing itself when it temporarily breaks down. Thus every learning experience is not only an invitation to improve our theories about the world; it is also an opportunity to improve our implicit theories about theory-building – to become a better learner. As we learn *how* to learn, by refining our repertoire of learning strategies, so we reduce the risk of being caught in a situation where we do not know what to do. We become able to plug the gaps in our competence faster and more safely.

What I am suggesting here is that an important part of development concerns a two-stage process: developing learning strategies within particular scripts; and then liberating those strategies, where applicable, for more general use. It thus becomes at least a possible goal for education to help these localized learning amplifiers to become disentangled from their original contexts, and to come to form a more powerful, transportable and flexible set of learning strategies. As this happens, the learner acquires more intelligence, in the sense of 'the ability to do something sensible when you don't know what to do'. Disembedded learning strategies are a very special group of minitheories: the ones that enable people to go beyond their learning in specific domains to handle a much greater variety of problems and unknowns. Instead of being restricted to paddling in the shallow waters that lie off islands of competence, we are able to build deep-sea drilling rigs, use submarines and construct long piers and inter-island bridges. When we cannot find the stepping stones we are no longer stumped; we can swim or row instead.

I have introduced the idea of learning strategies, or learning amplifiers, in the context of young children's learning, for this is where they must begin. But school at all levels presupposes learning abilities that are more complex than imitation. In the rest of this chapter I am going to look at some of the strategies that learners possess, or may not possess but might need, to cope effectively with the situation that confronts them in lessons. In doing so we will begin to tie this general psychological analysis back into the realities of school pupils' lives. The focus now will be on illustrating some of the requisite strategies. I shall leave until Chapter 8 the issue of the conditions that generally foster their *growth*.

SOCIAL LEARNING STRATEGIES

Many of the strategies that will be of use in the classroom are those which will have been developed during years of experience of less formal social encounters. Pre-eminent will be those that are used in the comprehension of spoken and written language. When understanding proceeds easily, as it does when we are having a relaxed conversation with friends, we are not even aware of the complex processing that is taking place. We have to identify the words they are using; look up their meaning or meanings; resolve ambiguities by seeing what other meanings are also being received; check the grammar of the sentences so that the meanings are fitted together in the right way; work out what pronouns like 'it' or 'they' are referring to; fill in gaps or implications by adding in appropriate pieces of our own general knowledge; relate the developing conversation to the non-verbal or social script within which it is taking place; and draw on our knowledge of the person to whom we are speaking in order to interpret what they are saying and to pitch our own responses appropriately.[4]

By the time people have reached adolescence they are nearly all virtuosi in this respect, and have learnt to generalize their skills to the one-sided, but actually quite similar, situations of reading informal material like comics, magazines and novels, and of listening to the radio and watching TV.[5] Soap operas and disc jockeys provoke activities that are like two-way conversations because such an important part of their appeal is that one must like or dislike the characters and generate opinions about them. When *Neighbours* fans meet, these opinions can then be used to form the basis of real conversations. In all these contexts, as we have seen, the emphasis is not so much on retaining a complete, accurate record of what was said, as on following the general drift and being ready to respond with judgements, preferences and thoughts of one's own.

Strategies of a variety of different sorts are developed in order to aid the accumulation and trading of social knowledge. Learning how to get into a conversation, and how to take turns at talking, is important, as is the ability to display what one knows or thinks in an entertaining fashion. For many adolescents, developing the skills of repartee and banter are seen as vital, and to be left flabbergasted or without a witty comeback can feel like significant social failure. One social learning strategy we might single out is collecting: being on the look-out for unusual or noteworthy events that fall in the general area of one's own and one's peer group's interests. The occurrences that grab attention are not all of those that are strange or informative, but those that are interesting in terms of one's personal web of social knowledge and understanding. These may include, in lessons, what one's friends are up to, and slips of the tongue by the teacher.

When children enter primary school they will be well on the way with these strategies and busy developing them during unsupervised encounters with each other, both in and out of the classroom. But the new process they will start, and which continues through secondary schooling, is one of tailoring and developing these social skills into strategies that are appropriate to the special demands of school. As they progress they will develop particular variants for talking to teachers (both particular teachers and in general) and for group work, class discussion, surreptitious chortling, mucking about and so on. The course and the success of this development will depend on a host of factors including pupil personality, teacher personality, teaching style, school ethos, pupils' cultures and sub-cultures and such important social influences on development as race, gender and class.

THE FORMAT OF LESSON FILES

Although the automatic, social strategies for understanding language are necessary for pupils to grasp the content of lessons, they are often not sufficient. Lessons regularly contain intellectual ideas and information that cannot be picked up so easily. So they also have to adapt, if they are to be 'successful students', to organizing what they learn in a different way. As we saw in Chapter 4, much of their informal social knowledge, and the language used to express it, is not, and does not need to be, at all systematic. The point is not that it is coherent, accurate or deeply understood, but that one can talk about it informally.

However, in all school subjects there are 'right' ways of thinking and talking that do not easily arise from, or adhere to, the informal patchwork of social knowledge that students bring with them. Curriculum knowledge is often required to be systematic, explicit and abstract. If it is acquired rightly, the idea is that the different pieces will fit together in the learner's mind like a jigsaw puzzle, to make an expanding, general, powerful way of looking at an aspect of the world. This sort of knowledge is mostly expressed through formal kinds of discourse, what we called in Chapter 4 'lesson language'. Thus, to go back to our computer analogy, we might say that learners have to format their disks and files differently if they are to meet the demands of the overt curriculum.

For example, recent research has shown that students' informal minitheories usually contain some ideas that relate to science or maths topics (such as energy, motion, heat or evolution) but that these ideas do not provide an ideal foundation on which to build the superstructure of 'lesson knowledge'.[6] Young people (and many adults, in fact) believe that for something to move there must be a force on it, and that an ice-cream wrapped in a blanket melts faster than one wrapped in aluminium foil.

These beliefs give rise to intuitions that conflict with scientific theories or observations. They can release into students' minds everyday associations and meanings that serve to confuse the student. They are stored, as we have seen, in a way that, while perfectly adequate for socializing, is much less abstract and coherent than the conceptual structure of formal science and maths. And the associated strategies for acquisition are also much more illogical and unsystematic and less directed towards sustained concentration on specific, difficult topics or problems. Thus, to do the 'brain-work' required by school demands the development of the inclination and confidence to grapple with material that is hard to understand or remember; the skills and strategies for doing so; and the mastery of new formats for recording what is learnt.

When faced with such material, learners have a number of options. They can search for sense and coherence in the hope that the effort will be repaid with an integrated structure of comprehension. They can give up seeking meaning and opt instead for verbatim retention of what seem to be key points. They can abandon even rote learning and apply, inefficiently, social learning strategies that may write on to a social knowledge file catchy fragments of the lesson. They can give up completely and switch into reverie or rebellion. We are now in a position to explore each of these options in more detail.

INTELLECTUAL LEARNING STRATEGIES

To do well in school, pupils need to be effective gatherers, organizers, integraters and expressers of knowledge. The main channels for gathering knowledge in school are listening, reading, asking questions and discussing. One essential strategy here is concentrating, by which I mean the vital ability to continue to focus on the topic, even though the words or ideas may not yet make good sense, and not switching off prematurely. Intellectual understanding arrives in different ways, depending on the material. Sometimes one bolts pieces on to a clear framework one after another, so that, for a successful student, the sense of clarity and mastery is present most of the time. Much of mathematics learning is potentially of this sort, and it is this intrinsic property of the subject that makes it so easy to fail at. Once you have failed to cross one of the chasms of understanding, it is very hard to make sense of whatever follows. But perhaps more typically, a grasp on a subject emerges more holistically after a period in an intellectual fog that may be quite protracted. (This sense of 'beginning to see the light' or of one's knowledge 'coming together' is often experienced by students only as they revise for examinations, if at all.) Continuing to attend while feeling befogged seems to be a strategy that successful students have learnt.[7]

Another important strategy for gathering knowledge is note-taking, about which (as for many of the strategies we will be reviewing in this section) much has been written in the expanding literature, both popular and scholarly, on 'study skills'. An especially important sub-skill of note-taking is being sensitive to the teacher's intonation and other forms of emphasis that signal the key points in what she is saying. In acquiring school knowledge the essential intention is to seek structure, and the key points provide foci around which the structure can be elaborated. To know what to write down, and how best to represent it, so that the deficiencies of memory are overcome, means that you have a record of what the homework was, for example, as well as of some of the information you will need to complete it. Even when teachers see their role in less didactic terms, these skills of pinpointing and recording essential information remain very important.

More generally, successful intellectual learners seem to adopt a stance of active interaction with the teacher and the topic. In 'study skills' or 'speed reading' courses, participants are urged to practise reading with a greater attitude of 'conversation' with the author – reviewing their own expectations of the material, thinking critically about what the book or article title, chapter and section headings mean, and formulating the questions that they want the text to answer.[8] They are told to read flexibly, suiting their speed to the nature of different materials and the purposes for which they are reading. Academic texts may need to be read slowly and carefully; a thriller can be skimmed. (It is possible to get this wrong, however. Woody Allen said somewhere, 'I took a speed-reading course once. It was fantastic. I read *War and Peace* in half an hour. It's about Russia.') This active engagement is an outgrowth of the 'arguing with the TV' habit that most young people, as we saw earlier, have developed already, but which many do not spontaneously transfer to the harder brain-work of school. It provides another example of the way in which abilities that were developed in one context for one purpose can evolve, if the conditions are right, into skills that have different functions in different contexts. By the same token, such potential resources will remain unrealized if the conditions for their metamorphosis are *not* present.

For intellectually difficult material an active approach does seem to be the best strategy – arguing with the writer, writing down thoughts and notes as you go along, trying to put things in your own words, and coming back to the most difficult parts again at the end, rather than getting 'blocked' on them when they first occur. Like all learning strategies, however, these need to be practised and encouraged, so that the learner can build up the ability and confidence to use them. It is not sufficient merely to tell students to adopt such a stance: they need to gain experience with it, and to be 'coached' by a teacher who can help them to see its utility for themselves.

An important component of this active stance is the ability to detect and build up structure in the material being studied. Trying to boil down everything you know about a topic to one sheet of paper, or to a set of headings, is a common feature of revision advice. A technique that some people find very useful is to take these headings and arrange them in a kind of 'map' (sometimes called mind-maps, spider diagrams or organic diagrams) that shows their relationships to each other.[9] Figure 6.1 shows a partial map that links together some of the ideas in this book.

One thing that seems to distinguish successful from unsuccessful students is the ability to recognize and articulate what it is that they do not know, or do not understand.[10] If one is able to see what the difficulty is, one can focus on it oneself, trying to retrieve and mobilize different pieces of existing knowledge that might be helpful; or one can formulate a sensible question to ask someone else. But students who are floundering at school lack the skill, and the confidence, to do this. They feel at sea, without any sense of a base of understanding to hang on to and to move out from. A learner in this state can be recognized by a glazed or miserable expression, an air of withdrawal and the plaintive (or defiant) cry, 'I just don't get it'. Switching off or mucking about may be self-preserving escapes from this hopeless and uncomfortable intellectual fix.

As I have just mentioned, the skill of being articulate about intellectual knowledge provides an important strategy for amplifying that knowledge. If you can talk to your teachers, or your Mum and Dad, or most importantly your friends, about school work, you may be in a much more powerful position than those who cannot[11] – although some students manage to be successful on their own. So articulacy is an ingredient of the ability to be a successful school student for two reasons: it actually helps you to learn and understand as well as providing you with the ability to express what you know, come exam time, or during discussions and tests. Unfortunately, it is sometimes assumed that expressing what one knows is relatively unproblematic and that

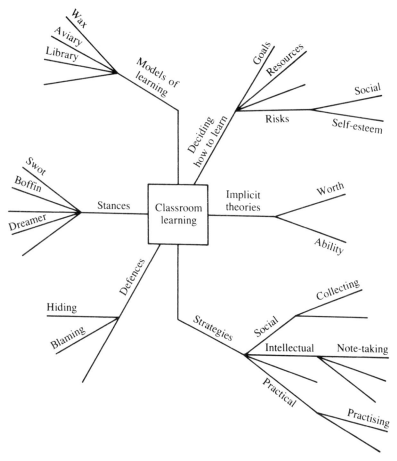

Figure 6.1. A partial mind-map for learning.

the major difficulties of learning occur only at the acquisition stage. Yet we are all familiar, even professors of philosophy I suspect, with the frustrating experience of not being able to 'find the right words' to express our thoughts. There is no reason to suppose that adolescents do not experience the same difficulty.

Just as flexibility is desirable for studying different kinds of material in different ways, so a variety of modes of expression is most useful, not the insistence that a specific 'register' is the appropriate response in all situations. Thus the kind of language that pupils use in the playground is fine for that context, and they might well jeopardize their social standing if they were suddenly to start spouting Queen's English. (Children who move schools often experience the discomfort of discovering that their 'posh' or 'common' or 'German' accents may give rise to teasing or worse, until they can learn to talk in a way that does not make them conspicuous.) However it is useful, for dealing with examiners and bureaucrats at least, to be able to switch into different modes when they are required. Even within school, different styles are encouraged, from 'creative writing' in an English lesson, to literal translation in French, to the formal framework of a scientific write-up or a geometric proof. There are different kinds of 'lesson language' to be mastered. Some youngsters arrive in secondary schools skilled in some of these and needing guidance in developing others. Other young people are less well equipped by their upbringings with language skills that can be readily tailored to the demands of lessons, and they will need more time, and perhaps more help, if the requisite voices are to develop at all.

Strategies for grappling with intellectual knowledge – knowledge that is more abstract, and more coherent, but for that very reason more difficult to grasp, than everyday social knowledge – start to be developed at primary school, but it is during the first few years of secondary school that the specialized skills of sustained thinking, of deliberate retention and of disciplined intellectual discussion are becoming more and more crucial. Some young people are more successful than others at crafting a viable repertoire of intellectual learning strategies out of their informal techniques for acquiring social and working knowledge. Those who manage it will be equipped thereby to do well in the public examinations. Those who fail to achieve the necessary evolution of their learning power – who cannot concentrate, sift out and record what is important, express their views clearly, remember what they do not understand – will be prohibited thereby from making further progress up the ladder of intellectual understanding and academic achievement.

VERBATIM LEARNING STRATEGIES

The third set of learning strategies, smaller than the previous two but of special relevance in school, comprises those that deliver verbatim knowledge. Such knowledge is sought in two kinds of situation: those where the task clearly requires it, and those where understanding is difficult and the student decides to stop trying to find a meaning and to fall back on to rote learning of (hopefully) the key points. Examples of the first kind would include learning a part in a play, the words of a song or a prayer, or the steps in a ritual. (No one would pay to hear an actor begin Hamlet's soliloquy with: 'Well, just between you and me, I'm a bit in two minds about this . . .'.) In the second case the learner decides that it is not worth persisting with the quest for real understanding because she does not have the time, resources, background knowledge or support, or because the benefits are not important enough to warrant the effort and/or risk entailed. This decision may or may not be a good one, as we shall see in Chapter 7.

In practice, pupils often have difficulty in building up the jigsaw puzzle as the different pieces are presented to them, and have to fall back on collecting them (perhaps by scribbling down notes as fast as they can while the teacher talks) rather than integrating them. This sort of verbatim knowledge is disintegrated and piecemeal. It resembles a pile of bricks rather than a well-designed house. And because it is not integrated into an expanding framework of comprehension, it is less easy to retrieve and use. Its applicability remains closely tied to the form in which, and the purposes for which, it was learnt. When those conditions are exactly repeated, verbatim knowledge may resurface, but otherwise it remains relatively inaccessible and useless. Its main functions in school are to help one pass tests on what one does not understand, and to retain formulae, definitions, vocabulary, etc. that have to be learnt by rote before they can be incorporated into a more meaningful framework. Rote learning is therefore a set of strategies that has a specific but very narrow sphere of utility. There is nothing 'wrong' with using rote learning, or encouraging its use, provided only that it is being used appropriately, and that the mental product that it delivers will be equal to the eventual task.

If pupils are going to continue to use verbatim learning in school, and school to reward it, it seems odd to fail to teach them explicitly the range of verbatim strategies that are known to be effective. These include scripting, imagery, chunking, acronyms and self-testing.[12] Scripting means making up a story or using a familiar one within which to embed strings of things that do not seem to fit together meaningfully. Imagery is known to be a powerful way of making associations, however bizarre, between seemingly unassociated things. Chunking means trying to lump together unrelated words, symbols, etc., by finding some common characteristic that sub-groups of them share. Acronyms are ways of associating things together via their initial letters (like PA MEND V TRAMS for the common French verbs that 'take *être*': *partir*, *aller*, *mourir*, *entrer* and so on. All these strategies rely on the general principle that it is useful to supplement relatively meaningless information with some sort of meaningful adhesive from one's own experience whilst learning, even if that adhesive does not give rise to any truly meaningful integration of the elements. Providing structure and coherence of any sort increases the likelihood of being able to find the information again when it is needed.

The final strategy in this short list, self-testing, increases the power of the traditional strategy for verbatim learning – repeating things over and over in your head. Self-testing (or better still, doing it with a friend) involves giving yourself part of the information to be learnt (a French word on one side of a card, say) and then trying to recall the rest of it (the English equivalent written on the back). Then you give yourself the answer. A good variant is to work through a stack of such cards, repeatedly discarding the ones you get right each time, until there are none left.[13] Perhaps more obviously than with the other types of learning, the ability to remember verbatim is a learnt one, and has nothing to do with any supposed general 'ability' or 'intelligence'. Yet it is surprisingly rarely that pupils are trained in the use of these simple tools.

PRACTICAL LEARNING STRATEGIES

So far we have focused on the kinds of learning strategy that are most necessary in the secondary school. But alongside these intellectual forms of learning there are other, more physical and practical kinds, which complement them, and which were the preponderant ones earlier in the child's life. Alongside the search for intellectual and verbatim knowledge, both structured and unstructured time in school involves the acquisition of considerable 'working knowledge'. If much school work involves adding to the language part of minitheory TALEs, practical learning requires modification of tendencies and appearances. In science lessons there are physical skills of weighing and measuring to be learnt; in art, techniques of painting; in French, some tricky new speech sounds; in technology and design, skills of making and shaping. Working knowledge guides (and often feels as if it actually resides in) our hands and feet and spontaneous ways of perceiving and responding. Verbal knowledge has to become dissolved in these subtle, tacit systems of muscular and perceptual control if one is to make the transition from pundit to practitioner. Thus the basic strategy for acquiring working knowledge is to try things out and to be alert to the results.[14] All our practical learning strategies are way of amplifying this basic competence by producing more sophisticated ideas about what to try out. They include the following.

Imitating is as useful a strategy for adolescents and student teachers as it is for infants. It involves watching how someone else, judged to be more expert than oneself, goes about the job, and then endeavouring to do it the same way. This is a useful source of ideas for developing all sorts of skills from diving, using a lathe or dancing to telling jokes or introducing oneself to people at discos. But it must be used cautiously, for the processes by which the performance is produced cannot be automatically inferred or adopted, and they have to be integrated with one's natural range of habits and attitudes. If the model is copied too closely, without allowing this integration to occur, it can become an act that is patently false and the desired effect will not be forthcoming.

Involving other people more directly as coaches is also helpful if they are willing and able to provide maxims or feedback. Maxims are rules of thumb, distilled out of others' competence, that can be used to direct and/or evaluate one's own developing performance. They are especially useful in the early stages of learning when one's own 'feel' for what is successful, or at least on the right track, is not yet well formed and one is therefore not very good at being self-correcting.[15] As expertise develops, it is often the case that the maxims are outgrown and can be disobeyed with profit rather than risk, so that there is no contradiction in scuba-diving instructors, say, telling beginners 'Never hold your breath under water' while themselves using breath-holding as a way of altering their buoyancy whilst submerged.

The way that experts give correction or feedback is also crucial, for the ideal is to provide specific suggestions ('mini-maxims', we might call them) about how performance can be improved without at the same time demoralizing the learners and making them feel depressed, inadequate or hopeless. An insensitive teacher-tutor, for example, may have this effect on a student teacher by reeling off at the end of an observed lesson twenty insightful criticisms of the lesson planning and conduct. Tutors may also fail to realize that students have to test their wisdom, to see if it is appropriate for their own personality and values. What works for one person, especially in such a complex skill as teaching, may not be the best solution for another.

Most important perhaps are the strategies that learners can use to amplify their own learning, independently of a tutor. Often these will come into their own once the rudiments of the ability have been mastered and a platform of confidence established. At this point deliberately experimenting with slightly different ways of performing an action can reveal alternative paths to achieving it that may be more economical and elegant, or may be better suited to different environments (remember the E in HEAD again).

More generally, experimenting underlies the ability to be resourceful and innovative in the face of novel or changing conditions. Teachers, especially but not exclusively student teachers, are forever encountering situations where their existing ways of construing or reacting let them down, and the strategy of generating a few new things to try out next time is essential if they are to become autonomous without feeling blocked or stuck. And pupils have to keep experimenting in order to get a good result for their science practicals or to win popularity.

The complement to experimenting is practising, which is the strategy of focusing on repeating, consolidating and automating a response that has been successful. Often when we 'get it right', we are unable to specify precisely what it was that we did, and for a while control is variable and success precarious. Practising integrates the components of successful action so that we can hit the bull's-eye, solve the differential equation or get the pastry crisp every time.

THE RIGHT STRATEGY FOR THE JOB

With learning strategies, as with all minitheories, learners need not only to have developed the content of their TALEs but also to have refined their HEADs. To the extent that the heading is inaccurate, the learner will be inclined to try to use the strategy in situations where it will not work, or will fail to perceive its relevance in situations where it would have been successful. It is no use trying to reason your way to becoming a better teacher. It is probably no use trying to solve the problem of whether to have a child by asking the Citizens Advice Bureau. You will not find out the time of the next train to York by sitting down and meditating.

A large part of students' difficulty in maths, for example, is caused by an unclear grasp of the extent and limits of use of a particular operation.[16] Students may persist in saying that $\frac{3}{4} + \frac{1}{3} = \frac{4}{7}$ not so much because they cannot use the correct procedures as because they have not learnt to distinguish functionally between integers and fractions, and therefore have no intuitive, spontaneous sense of the quite definite 'range of convenience' that the *add* 'program' has. (Actually, things become even more complicated still, for it is not true to say that you can never get the right answer by adding the tops and adding the bottoms of fractions. If an exam consists of two parts, one out of 30 marks, on which Jill scores 26, and the second out of 70, on which she scores 44, it is quite correct to calculate her overall performance as $\frac{26}{30} + \frac{44}{70} = \frac{70}{100}$. It is not impossible that an infuriated maths teacher could be scribbling 'You can't add fractions like this' on a student's exam – and then calculating the marks in just the forbidden way!)

The questions that teachers face, if they are interested in helping pupils to develop their sense of the appropriateness of the learning strategies they possess, mirrors the one we looked at in Chapter 5: do they know what the future situation, in which they want the learning strategy to become available, is going to look like, or not? If they do, then their task is to recreate in the learning situation, as closely as possible, the conditions in and purposes for which the learning is eventually to be used. If your predominant goal is to get your students to do well in a predictable kind of examination, set them timed questions, go through past papers, coach them in exam technique and give plenty of mock exams.

However if, as is often the case, teachers cannot specify what the context and the task are going to be that pupils will have to face, and therefore want to give them knowledge and skill in as flexible and generalizable a form as possible, then other conditions must be used. We cannot, it should now be clear, just cross our fingers and hope that this will happen. We have to build into pupils' learning experiences frequent opportunities for them to *discover* the range and limitations of what they are learning, through self-directed experimentation with it. Such opportunities cannot be premeditated, and they therefore introduce untidiness into the syllabus. But if we try to short-circuit this process of discovery it will not happen, and what pupils have learnt is likely to remain locked up in its little school-based minitheories. It will not 'come to mind' on subsequent occasions when it might be useful.

METAPHOR

Finally in this chapter I want to mention some of the 'higher' strategies that people can develop to help them handle unfamiliar concepts and material. The first one, very beneficial for getting started in new domains, especially when first encountering new areas of intellectual knowledge, is the use of metaphor. Metaphors provide a way of structuring new domains that depends not on the particular content of an existing file, but on the system of relationships that may have been established within such a minitheory. Using a metaphor is like taking an established minitheory, stripping it of most of its content and floating it into a new area, the domain of the problem, like a drilling rig. The metaphor provides a vantage point from which the puzzle may begin to make sense.

To say that electricity in a circuit is like water in a loop of pipes provides a way of conceptualizing the relationships between voltage, current and resistance that can help to make a beginning in intellectual understanding. The pitfall, of course, is that students may unwittingly copy into the new file aspects of the metaphor that are irrelevant or inaccurate, and these, if unrecognized by both learner and teacher, can form a barrier to the flexible adaptation of the file that the nature of the new domain will eventually require. (James Thurber describes his grandmother who 'lived the latter years of her life in the horrible suspicion that electricity was dripping invisibly all over the house'.[17]) If teachers deliberately use metaphor to introduce a new topic, it will be part of their responsibility to anticipate such misunderstandings, to map carefully the points that correspond and those that do not, and to announce clearly when the original ladder must be kicked away in order for further understanding to develop.

LOGIC

As we acquire knowledge, particularly intellectual and social knowledge, so it becomes integrated into a constantly expanding network of understanding. This will contain many more implications to be drawn, and associations to be made, than are discovered explicitly at the time of original learning. Logic and fantasy are two different but complementary strategies for uncovering these latent links. Logical thought is a powerful way of sucking out of our verbal knowledge implications that are buried within it. But note that, for this to happen, the file on which the knowledge is stored must itself contain a logic sub-routine as part of its TALE. Either that, or something must cause us to switch to such a routine at the same time as the knowledge is active. If neither of these conditions apply, it will appear as if we are 'unable' to think logically in this domain.

In just the same way, maths provides a powerful strategy for exploring the relationships between quantities. But if there is no maths sub-routine copied on to the physics minitheory, or if the teacher does not explicitly signal when a 'disk-change' is required, then all the maths that students know in maths lessons will appear (mysteriously!) to have been forgotten during physics. This lack of transfer of skills between subjects is frequently lamented by teachers, but it is to be expected within the present framework, where changes of stance (and therefore frequently of available knowledge-base) from situation to situation are bound to occur.

FANTASY

Fantasy – the active use of imagination – is another useful strategy for pushing out the limits of what we know, and seeing what happens. The implications and applications of existing knowledge that are uncovered are of a much more loose-weave, intuitive nature than those of logic, being based on social, working and implicit forms of knowledge rather than intellectual. In many areas these intuitions turn out to be more subtle and accurate than logical deductions because they are able to draw on vast areas of inarticulate knowledge that cannot be manipulated rationally.

Conversely, there are other areas where logic delivers better answers than imagination. For example, imagine the earth as a smooth sphere and that round the equator there is tied snugly a non-elastic piece of string. If the string is cut, six feet added and the 'slack' now spaced equally so that a constant gap exists between string and earth all the way round, how big is the gap? Most people's strong intuition is that it is tiny, say a millimetre or less, whereas simple geometry proves that it must be just under a foot. It is interesting that 'working knowledge' continues to assert its intuition even after 'intellectual knowledge' has examined and accepted the proof.[18]

When we describe people as 'intuitive' or 'rational' types, what we are ascribing to them is a degree of preference for, and/or skill at using, the elaboration strategies of fantasy and logic respectively. We are not talking about innate traits of character but about learnt habits with which people may have become stuck, but which are always potentially open to development and reappraisal. With the exception of art, music, drama and some approaches to teaching literature, secondary schools are generally characterized by the pervasive attempt to equip adolescents to be rational whilst ignoring the possibility of helping them to become more skilful in their use of imagination and intuition.

SELF-AWARENESS

Perhaps the most general level of learning strategies are those that are concerned with self-appraisal, and that provide an array of checks for determining how one's learning is progressing. Most basic is monitoring one's actions and their consequences to see exactly what happens and how it is different from one's expectations about what would happen. The more accurate one's monitoring – the better data one collects about the situation – the more precise and discriminating can be one's response, and the more rapidly one will develop to the point of renewed and expanded mastery. Monitoring refers not only to observation of external consequences, but also to one's internal responses of feeling. Awareness of one's own reactions to events (such as 'It worked but I didn't like myself for shouting that way' or 'Despite what I thought, too much noise really does upset me') forms an integral part of the data that serve to guide learning in the direction of an expertise that is ideally both effective and personally congenial and satisfying.

Other strategies for self-appraisal include checking, estimating and reflecting. Checking is the intellectual equivalent of monitoring: it is the strategy of evaluating one's understanding or solution to a problem in terms of the constraints and goals with which one started. Students who are not very successful at maths, for example, are often poor checkers.[19] They look at a problem, choose a program for tackling it, feed the data into the program and assume (or hope) that the first answer that emerges must be the right one. More successful students tend at this point to 'jump up a level' from the details of problem-solving to check that the answer 'fits' with the original problem. Estimating is an important adjunct strategy here for checking on the plausibility of the solution – is it the right kind of answer? Is it sensible, in terms of my general knowledge (if I have concluded that the bath takes 0.0037 seconds to fill, or the car 7.4×10^6 days to complete its journey)?

Finally, reflecting is a more leisurely kind of appraisal of things recently learnt, 'off-line' rather than 'on-line' in computer terms, in which points of congruence, overlap or conflict are sought, and where possible tidied up. For example, if one has developed on-line a series of little purpose-built skills to do a variety of different jobs, reflection may uncover some underlying similarity of operation that enables a more powerful, general-purpose procedure to be written instead. Annette Karmiloff-Smith, for example, has shown how young children spontaneously use a mixture of reflecting and experimenting to search for greater generalization and coherence in what they have already learnt.[20]

SUMMARY AND READING

Learning strategies amplify our ability to solve problems and accelerate our acquisition of expertise. The earliest arise through a process of 'spawning', when a routine that has developed within a particular minitheory is discovered to have the potential to aid learning, and is progressively liberated from its parent context. Later strategies may be more deliberately indicated or exemplified. Children's pre-school repertoire of social learning strategies forms the basis for the evolution of the more specialized set that will be required for school success. Some children have a rich and appropriate repertoire; others do not, and are consequently at risk of floundering. All children face problems in learning to 'format' their knowledge in a variety of initially unfamiliar ways, and ignoring these problems may lead to a breakdown in the evolution of more intellectual learning abilities. The increased emphasis in schools on the development of skills has changed but not lessened these difficulties. Time to integrate and experiment with skills is vital if they are to develop broad, spontaneous utility. Rote learning has a small but useful sphere of operation which must be understood if it is not to be misapplied. Metaphor, fantasy, logic and reflective self-awareness can all be seen as higher-level learning amplifiers. I have used the notion of a 'learning strategy' very broadly, to cover specific techniques as well as these more general abilities.

A good explanation of the 'higher level' sense is provided by John Nisbet and Janet Shucksmith's *Learning Strategies*. This is especially good on the failure of less subtle approaches to teaching 'study skills'. The best accounts of trying to teach, in schools, in such a way that awareness, monitoring and so on are deliberately strengthened, are contained in a book edited by John Baird and Ian Mitchell, *Improving the Quality of Teaching and Learning*.

Strategies of intellectual learning are reviewed in *Cognitive Strategies and Educational Performance,* edited by J. R. Kirby, and in *Learning Strategies,* edited by H. F. O'Neill. They are related to the school curriculum in a Schools' Council paper by Michael Marland. Still one of the best introductions to the education of intuitive skills is Michael Polanyi's *Personal Knowledge.*[21]

NOTES

(1) Samuel Butler (1971) *The Way of All Flesh.* Harmondsworth: Penguin.

(2) The notion of 'attunement' comes from Stern, D. N. (1985) *The Interpersonal World of the Infant: A View from Psychoanalysis and Developmental Psychology.* New York: Basic Books.

(3) Kelly, G. (1955) *The Psychology of Personal Constructs.* New York: W. W. Norton.

(4) Clark, H. and Clark, E. (1977) *Psychology and Language.* New York: Harcourt Brace Jovanovich. Garnham, A. (1988) *Artificial Intelligence.* London: Routledge. Claxton, G. L. (1984) *Live and Learn: An Introduction to the Psychology of Growth and Change in Everyday Life.* London: Harper & Row, chapter 4; reissued (1988) Milton Keynes: Open University Press.

(5) Ryder, N. (1983) *Television, Science and Adolescence.* London: Independent Broadcasting Authority.

(6) Driver, R. (1984) *The Pupil as Scientist.* Milton Keynes: Open University Press. Osborne, R. J. and Freyberg, P. (1985) *Learning in Science.* Auckland, New Zealand: Heinemann. Black, P. and Lucas, A. (eds) (1990) *Children's Informal Ideas in Science.* London: Routledge.

(7) Marton, F., Hounsell, D. and Entwistle, N. (1984) *The Experience of Learning.* Edinburgh: Scottish Academic Press.

(8) See, for example, Morton, J. (1966) A two-hour rapid-reading course. *Nature,* **211,** 323–4.

(9) Buzan, T. (1974) *Use Your Head.* London: BBC Publications.

(10) Holt, J. (1984) *How Children Fail,* revised edn. Harmondsworth: Penguin.

(11) See Turner, G. (1983) *The Social World of the Comprehensive.* Beckenham, Kent: Croom Helm.

(12) See Howe, M. J. A. (1984) *A Teacher's Guide to the Psychology of Learning.* Oxford: Blackwell, for a fuller description of these strategies.

(13) A suggestion of John Holt's in *How Children Fail,* op. cit.

(14) As we saw earlier, this seems to be part of our endowment of natural learning ability, as described in the entertaining book by Gallwey, T. (1975) *The Inner Game of Tennis.* London: Cape.

(15) This is well described by Skinner, B. F. (1974) *About Behaviorism*. London: Cape.

(16) See, for example, Hart, K. M. (1981) *Children's Understanding of Mathematics*. London: John Murray.

(17) James Thurber, *My Life and Hard Times*; reprinted in *The Thurber Carnival* (1984). Harmondsworth: Penguin.

(18) Try it! If you cannot work it out for yourself, see Claxton, *Live and Learn*, op. cit. p. 14.

(19) Hart, *Children's Understanding of Mathematics*, op. cit.

(20) Karmiloff-Smith, A. Children's problem-solving. In Lamb, M. E., Brown, A. L. and Rogoff, B. (eds) (1984) *Advances in Developmental Psychology*, vol. III. Hillsdale, NJ: Erlbaum.

(21) Nisbett, J. and Shucksmith, J. (1986) *Learning Strategies*. London: Routledge & Kegan Paul. Baird, J. R. and Mitchell, I. J. (eds) (1986) *Improving the Quality of Teaching and Learning: An Australian Case Study – The PEEL Project*. Melbourne: Monash University Printery. Kirby, J. R. (ed.) (1984) *Cognitive Strategies and Educational Performance*. London: Academic Press. O'Neill, H. F. (ed.) (1978) *Learning Strategies*. New York: Academic Press. Marland, M. (1981) Information skills in the secondary curriculum. *Schools' Curriculum Bulletin*, **9**. London: Methuen. Polanyi, M. (1958) *Personal Knowledge*. London: Routledge & Kegan Paul.

Chapter 7

Learning to be in School

Jack: I know nothing, Lady Bracknell.

Lady Bracknell: I am pleased to hear it. I do not approve of anything that tampers with natural ignorance. Ignorance is like a delicate exotic fruit; touch it and the bloom is gone. The whole theory of modern education is radically unsound. Fortunately in England, at any rate, education produces no effect whatsoever.

Oscar Wilde[1]

So far we have focused on a range of strategies that pupils may have available, or may need to deploy, to meet the demands of the classroom. These strategies are good for different situations and for different jobs. Some of them focus on the content of the lesson and are designed to deliver either comprehension or retention of the subject matter. Others relate more to acquiring particular skills. But not all learning strategies, as we have seen, are focused on the 'official business' of the classroom. Some of them are directed more towards people and their interactions – they enable pupils to learn about the teacher and each other, to get a sense of 'what goes' within the culture of a particular class or in the presence of a particular teacher, and to pick up information that will enable their interactions to proceed smoothly and successfully.

Pre-existing social learning strategies are not only fashioned into a tool-kit for tackling the overt curriculum; they also need to be directed towards the problems inherent in a very particular social predicament. Many of these problems are personal and emotional, so that, in addition to learning strategies, there is an important set of *defensive* strategies, which we shall look at later in this chapter, that are directed towards maintaining self-esteem, or the esteem of others, in the face of what look like intellectual or social threats of various sorts.

From the teachers' point of view, the classroom is most commonly thought of as a place where particular learning tasks make contact with a number of different brains. The goal is to help some kind of predetermined learning to occur inside a collection of individual heads. But from the learners' perspective, things are not so neat. Their overriding concern is to make sense of a complex predicament that is quite as much social and emotional as it is intellectual. The situation that pupils meet in a classroom is an intricate mixture of demands and opportunities. Their problem, therefore, is not to select a single strategy to respond to a single demand, but rather to develop a more general orientation towards the class, the subject and the teacher that allows them to integrate all the different kinds of constraint into a successful package of strategies for coping.

STANCES

In order to understand the way that pupils respond to the many facets of classroom life, we have to try to look at the situation that they face as a whole. In particular, we need to look at the ways in which the cognitive, emotional, motivational and sociocultural factors interact with each other. For the way in which individual learners approach the lesson content – the strategies they adopt towards it – will depend on their own more general goals and ambitions, on their perception of the opportunities available, and on social pressures that are created by the culture of the particular class. We need particularly to be aware that pupils' engagement with the official 'content' of a lesson will be a function of the way that they have decided to reconcile *all* the conflicting pressures and demands of the situation, and not merely of their 'ability' or their 'motivation'. It is necessary, in order for pupils to do well in a subject, for them to possess relevant learning strategies, but it is not sufficient. Those strategies must also form a central part of the overall plan that they have developed for coping with the situation. They may be perfectly capable of learning to read, for example, but be functionally unable (or unwilling) to do so in the presence of a particular teacher or peer group.

So as well as special-purpose strategies for learning, pupils must also develop more generalized *stances* towards lessons, and perhaps towards school as a whole. By 'stance' I mean a package of measures for dealing with the multifaceted predicament that a lesson represents. As stances are developed, so pupils acquire a set of dispositions and expectations which guide the way they perceive, attend, learn and behave. Pupils will differ in the particular stances they develop, in the range of stances they possess, and in the variability and flexibility with which they deploy them. At one end there are pupils who have a single stance towards school as a whole, which makes them impervious to the differences between subjects and teachers. At the other are those who are highly sensitive to those differences, and whose achievement, demeanour and attitude vary accordingly. In either case, the stance or stances chosen may be effective or ineffective.

Different stances do not refer to intrinsic aspects of learners' personalities, or even of their abilities, but to roles that they develop and adopt, perhaps quite consistently, perhaps with some variability, in order to meet their perceived needs within the perceived range of possibilities that the lesson offers, and in the light of the learners' own intuitive estimates of the resources that they themselves bring with them. All learners will have such stances, and much of their learning, as they go through school, involves creating, modifying and selecting between the stances that they have available. This learning is at least as prevalent and as important as the increase in knowledge or skill that arises from the application of learning strategies to lessons. School is not just a sort of neutral medium within which learning happens; it is an important predicament to be learnt *about*.

Let us look at some examples of these stances. I have created these examples by trying to imagine what the learning strategies might be that are associated with some of the common categories of pupil that have been revealed by ethnographic research.[2]

Swot stance

Pupils with a swot stance tend to show a mixture of compliance and unadventurousness. Their main motives are to keep out of trouble (avoid the threat of teacher disapproval or parental disappointment) and/or to get what they can from school in the way of exams. They may or may not be high achievers, but their orientation is towards the use of verbatim learning strategies with perhaps some relatively unquestioning comprehension. They see school, cognitively, as about the accumulation of knowledge which enables them to pass exams. In swot stance, therefore, students perceive copying down notes to be 'learnt', and doing textbook problems, as being 'proper learning', and tend to disparage or ignore aspects of lessons that do not conform to this image. When a teacher tries to enliven the lesson with interesting asides or embellishments, swot stance switches off, or complains after a short while, 'When are we going to do some work, Miss?', or asks suspiciously, 'Is this on the syllabus, Sir?'.

When eventually students who have been regularly in swot stance are confronted with an unexpected type of exam that requires them to 'think' (that is, to transfer their knowledge to new situations and/or deploy it more flexibly) they become indignant and complain that the test is 'unfair'. And quite understandably so, for they may well have been led by the style of their teacher, past exam papers and the ethos of the school, to back an approach to learning that has in this instance turned out to be a loser. In swot stance, pupils tend to adopt attitudes that have been called 'conformist' or 'compliant'.[3] Pupils who stay in swot stance for too long run the risk of being labelled 'teachers' pets', 'goodies', or 'browners' by their peers. McLaren, for example, quotes one pupil saying, 'I hate trying to act like a browner. But you can get away with it. If the teacher thinks you are trying to be a browner before exams, then you'll get better marks. But you might lose your friends if you stay a browner too long.'[4] Fuller, in her study of black girls in a London comprehensive school, notes of one group, 'The black girls conformed to the stereotype of the good pupil only in so far as they worked conscientiously at the schoolwork or homework set. But they gave all the appearances in class of not doing so.'[5]

Boffin stance

A boffin stance to school learning highlights and absorbs

intellectual knowledge about certain topics of interest to the learner. While the rest of the class is grappling with adding fractions, the boffin is privately reading her elder sister's A-level book on differential calculus under the desk. The learning strategies embedded in a boffin 'file' produce intense concentration and tenacity, without any sense of resistance or resentment, and deliver a formidable knowledge of the topic – often to the embarrassment of the teacher. An habitual boffin may do well or poorly in an examination, depending on whether 'her' topic comes up. She is likely to spend two hours answering one question brilliantly – and failing the test because seven questions should have been attempted. In extreme boffin stance, other adolescent goals such as peer approval, and the attendant concerns with being fashionable or popular, may be eclipsed, so that habitual boffins are treated with a kind of indulgent disdain by their more modish peers, being labelled in some schools as 'dippoes' or 'weirds'.[6] Boffin stance is often quite selective: someone who is a boffin in biology, may well be predominantly 'swot' in French, and intermittently 'dreamer' and 'socialite' in English.

Socialite stance

Socialite pupils may be less concerned about – or perhaps less hopeful of achieving – exam success than students in swot stance. They do not want or are not able to accumulate successfully either exam-passing or interest-satisfying knowledge. Instead socialites, when they are attending to the lesson content, use the same kinds of learning procedure that are used to collect social knowledge, where pieces of knowledge are picked up from casual conversation, watching TV or reading magazines or novels. This mode, as we have seen before, selects and highlights ideas or events that are attention-grabbing, and fits them rather loosely into a web of knowledge that is unsystematic and vernacular.

In lessons, socialites use minitheories that are derived from everyday, out-of-school experience. Such students are likely to be chatty and distractible, interested in 'stinks and bangs' or what French children have for breakfast, but rather at sea with the theory or the grammar. Their understanding of scientific terms such as 'compound' or 'solution' may be constantly confused by everyday meanings and associations that are not kept distinct. Students who have not evolved, or are not able to mobilize, effective strategies for accurate memory or understanding in the classroom often tend to fall back on using the undeveloped social strategies that this stance permits. To learn in this mode is to learn without sustained attention, without seeking coherence or integration, and without being concerned to appraise (spontaneously) what is learnt in any rational or empirical way. Instead the immediate social pressures and priorities lead to an unsystematic collection of ephemera.

In fact, as the name implies, pupils in this stance are at least as interested in personalities and interactions as they are in ideas. While keeping half an ear open to the teacher for instructions or information that makes little or no intellectual demands, or for interesting titbits or slips of the tongue, the remaining ear-and-a-half are tuned in to the social dynamics of the classroom. Socialite stance may vary from quiet, non-disruptive (but non-work-related) chatting between pairs or small groups of pupils up to the widely reported 'joker' variant. Beynon reports the fine divisions within the joker mode that are made by pupils themselves.[7] There are, for example, 'comedians' (witty), 'fools' (more physical, clowning), 'stupids' (whose attempts to be funny frequently misfire) and 'kids' (whose humour is judged immature by peers). In addition to the socialites who may not be achieving very well in terms of their schoolwork, Beynon's informants identified a clear category of 'good kids' (as distinct from 'goodies' or 'goody-goodies'), who are those who manage to combine swot and socialite into a successful style. Good kids are those who work hard and do not upset the teachers, but who at the same time are willing to 'have a joke'. They are also noted for their readiness to help their peers by offering explanations, sharing their own work, etc.

Dreamer stance

Some of the stances that pupils adopt towards lessons may not orient them towards the content of the lesson at all. For example, a student in dreamer stance is oriented not towards acquiring knowledge from the outside world, but towards the world of inner play and fantasy. Habitual dreamers may be very skilled at the productive use of fantasy and imagination, but will not usually have harnessed these intuitive learning strategies to the business of solving *intellectual* problems. (It is the ability to achieve this yoking of fantasy and intellect that often distinguishes the creative learner in a field. The history of science is replete with examples, from Einstein 'downwards'.)

External events may be sampled occasionally to see if anything interesting or even understandable is going on, though these brief snatches of 'reality' may be used only as prompts for further fantasy work. This is a common stance for students to switch into when they are not engaged with what is going on around them, and it has several potentially useful functions. It may insulate a student from the painful awareness that he is unable to grasp the content of a lesson, and thus provide an effective defence against the threat to self-esteem that persistent failure poses. For swots and boffins it may provide a temporary withdrawal from a lesson that seems to them (but for quite different reasons) to have gone off track. It provides for all young people a safe inner playground for experiments with identity, vocation or capability that could not be made overtly. And for some students it may provide an opportunity to do emotional 'work', especially on relationships with family and friends, that is actually more important to them at the moment than the value of pi, the meaning of a poem or the origins of volcanoes. Persistent dreamers may also try to become 'invisible' in the classroom so that their academic inadequacies are not exposed or their rich inner fantasies disrupted. These are the ones that a young friend of mine calls the 'radiator kids' because they have learnt that the best place not to be noticed is down the sides of the classroom by the radiators.

Rebel stance

The next member of this partial roll-call of classroom stances is the familiar rebel. The major goal of rebel stance is to attract approval and appreciation to oneself from the other pupils in the class, either by using a more challenging variant of the joker strategy – wisecracking and outwitting or confusing the teacher – or by adopting a directly confrontational stance, like that of 'mucker' or 'hardnut'.[8] This mode is often adopted by students defensively (like dreaming) against the experience of failure, but it is by no means exclusively a defence. Any student who has a perhaps transient but strong need for 'peer validation' may drop into rebel mode, even though she may have reasonable strategies for accumulating intellectual and verbatim knowledge. 'Bright' students who are rebel-jokers or muckers are often the most exasperating for a teacher to deal with. (I remember getting one report at school that said, 'Guy can do physics standing on his head – and often does'.) This stance selects and highlights opportunities for mischief and can be exquisitely sensitive to the possibilities of gas taps and to the existence of sexual *double entendres* in the most unlikely places.

DEFENDING STRATEGIES

I have indicated that these stances may be used defensively, or have a defensive component to them. Swots may be swotting in order to avoid having to compete in the market place of sexual banter, just as rebels may be, but are not necessarily, rebelling to avoid the ignominy of looking 'thick'. It is time to make explicit just how important and *valuable* defensiveness is as a complement to learning. When people encounter a new situation, one in which the best way of operating is not immediately clear, one approach is to apply learning strategies to it in the hope that understanding or mastery will result. But learning is not always the most intelligent response. Sometimes it makes better sense to decline the learning invitation and instead to escape from, avoid or in some other way defend against the situation. These defensive strategies are as vital a set of responses to strangeness as the learning strategies. In some situations novelty may well conceal physical danger – being bitten by a dog, or run over. In others, more common in the classroom and staffroom, the danger may be social – a sarcastic remark from a colleague, or sniggers from other pupils when one gives a 'stupid' answer. Thus the learner's problem involves deciding not only how and what to learn about in a lesson, but also whether to engage with one of the learning opportunities at all; and if not, how to defend oneself effectively.

Thus the stances that a person deploys in school may well contain defensive strategies, designed to ward off apparent threats, as well as, or instead of, learning strategies, whose function is to take up challenges. It may be useful to describe briefly here some of the defences that are encountered in school, in both classroom and staffroom.[9]

Leaving involves physically removing yourself from the source of threat or stress. Pupils bunk off, get sick and become 'school phobic'.[10] Teachers have 'virus infections', get seconded on courses, are promoted out of the classroom, leave the profession, or, if all else fails, obtain long-term sick leave.

Hiding, as practised by the 'radiator kids', involves endeavouring to make onself invisible in classroom or staffroom (often by sitting in the least noticed places and keeping still) so that threatening situations and encounters are minimized.

Tensing involves physically suppressing bad feeling by locking up parts of musculature that would otherwise quiver. When this becomes habitual it increases the likelihood of a host of psychosomatic aches and pains: proneness to minor illness and to digestive, respiratory, menstrual or eating disorders.[11]

Denying involves becoming tactically unconscious of what is going on around you. It is seen in teachers who bumble on oblivious to chaos and in pupils who are stunned when they fail despite numerous clear warnings.

Dulling means using narcotic or analgesic drugs to replace bad feeling with good, and tension with relaxation. Adolescents typically prefer non-prescription drugs and solvents at the moment; teachers opt in the main for tranquillizers and sleeping pills. Both groups use alcohol.

Depressing involves becoming tactically unconscious of what is going on inside you – in particular of bad feelings. This is not a very good strategy as the effort required to ignore oneself leaves you tired, listless, joyless – and depressed.[12]

Distracting involves filling up the 'space' left by tensing, denying or depressing with safer activity. At home both teachers and students may watch a great deal of TV and be inordinately distressed when it breaks down and they have to spend an evening without it. Teachers may distract themselves from deep concerns by making mountains out of molehills like the staffroom coffee fund or the standards of dress of colleagues. Pupils may distract themselves from the threat of failure by becoming dreamers, from the threat of insignificance by becoming rebels, or from the threat of unpopularity by becoming swots.

Regressing means not having to try, by virtue of denying capability and often by responding to requests to work with a mixture of helplessness ('You do it for me') and tantrum-like aggression ('How dare you ask me?'). Both adults and young people use this.

Blaming means not having to try, by virtue of denying responsibility. As well as making the 'victim' helpless, this strategy allows her a pleasurable serving of self-righteousness by pointing out how lazy, incompetent or recalcitrant other people are. Many pupils' 'excuses' are denials of responsibility,[13] which are often met with collusion by teachers.

Displacing is a variant of blaming where the righteous indignation or plain hostility is redirected at 'safer' others like spouse, own children, immigrants, little kids, toys, cat, football teams or car (irrational anger at mechanical failures frequently appears to be displaced blame). Bullying by both teachers and children is often a form of displacement.

Denigrating is another variant of blaming where it is specifically the learning event and the person responsible for it that is attacked. Adolescents who are having difficulty learning may blame the teacher, the material, the room and the activity ('This is stupid, Miss'; 'Mr Mandrake is a wally'). Teachers who are resisting change may attack the perceived origin, be it headteacher, County Hall or central government.

Rationalizing means explaining why you are a worthwhile, lovable person *really*, despite appearances to the contrary. It involves telling frequently lengthy hard-luck stories to anyone who will listen, in the hope of gaining their sympathy and exoneration.

Exaggerating is a useful addition to rationalizing, and involves inflating the awfulness of events in order to convince oneself (and others if they will stand still long enough) that nobody, however wonderful, could have coped in such dreadful circumstances – thus salvaging self-esteem.

Compensating involves spending considerable time doing things you can do well, in order not to have any time left to do the things you ought to do, but are afraid you will do badly. For example, some adolescents (e.g. 'boffins') and some teachers (e.g. 'workaholics') may be very busy avoiding their feared lack of success in relationships.

Specializing means forming a group of people who are the receivers of true wisdom – some esoteric approach to teaching, a fashion in clothes or music – which outsiders 'do not understand' and therefore cannot criticize. Being special, you can value your own activities and interests while looking down on your unenlightened peers and colleagues, without ever really having to explain what you are doing and why it is so great. Specializer teachers are often to be found running 'alternative courses' and 'special options' for pupils and students that seem based on passionately held but poorly articulated premises.

CHOOSING WHEN AND HOW TO LEARN

The basis of the whole approach to pupils' learning that we are exploring is that they have a variety of ways of confronting any learning opportunity. First they have to decide whether or not to accept the invitation, and they then have to select a way of going about learning or defending that seems to meet their needs and the needs of the situation. However pupils respond, they do so for what *to them* are good reasons. The reasons may not be obvious to someone else. They may not be obvious even to the learners, but they are there.

We now need to map out some of the considerations, derived both from empirical studies and from a more commonsense appraisal, of what factors might plausibly weigh in the learners' balance. What questions might they ask themselves, albeit tacitly, as they confront an opportunity to learn? As I have been stressing in this chapter – to balance the more intellectual emphasis of the earlier discussions – they are emotional and social, as well as more straightforwardly cognitive or motivational.

What are the perceived benefits of learning, and of learning in different ways?

If I were to remember, or try to understand, or seek for personal significance, or choose to muck about, what consequences might follow and how do these consequences match my own current set of needs, wants, interests, ambitions and goals? If I want to be a nuclear physicist, I may decide that not learning and mucking about will not do. If I want to be a hairdresser, then perhaps they will.

What am I eventually going to want or have to use this knowledge for?

What are my tacit assumptions about how I am going to display what I know? What is the context of eventual use of this learning, and what kind of structure or format will be appropriate? From the same lesson, boffin stance can select deep intellectual knowledge (in order to understand books from the local university library on unified field theory, and to converse with other boffins); swot stance can select the formulae and definitions; socialite stance can select what a foetal heart monitor is for and how useful it is, and retain nothing of the physics involved in its construction; and dreamer stance can take one look at a Bunsen burner and construct a ten-minute fantasy about concentration camps. This consideration will be influenced by the external task demands, if the learner has decided, even broadly, to play the game. What these demands actually are will be understood more or less clearly, and more or less accurately, depending on the expectations generated by the teachers' style of teaching (dictating notes versus rambling discussions) and testing (retention versus intelligent speculation), and on the entire set of social rituals and ethos that the classroom has developed.

What other priorities do I have, and how will different learning strategies affect them?

People's goals may be seen as parts of a large 'portfolio of priorities' that vary in their urgency. One of the decision-making questions therefore concerns how my choice will impinge on my other priorities. Can I find a way of both studying as hard as I can (to get a good GCSE grade) and mucking about a bit so that I do not get branded a 'melon' (one London school's name for the 'swots' because they are reputed to have large squishy heads)? Is being cool and defiant important enough to risk letters home and battles with my parents? What sacrifices will be involved (do I suppose) in making different choices? Do I have the time really to grapple with my maths when I especially want to do well in French and English? If I decide that (1) maths is too hard, (2) peer approval is important, (3) parental disapproval is not so important and (4) my asides usually make people laugh, then I might opt for a joker stance. If I decide that (1) maths is too hard, (2) peer approval is important but unlikely (I am not very good at being cool and witty) and (3) parental disapproval does matter, then I could opt for being a dreamer and a 'radiator kid', and hope that I can get away with being invisible.

What personal resources do I have to respond in different ways?

Do I have what it takes to get to medical school? What has my experience (especially of teachers' reactions) taught me about my 'ability' to understand or remember things? Can I get good enough grades (to pass exams, satisfy parents, keep out of trouble) by revising hard at the last minute? How good am I at making mischief while remaining undetected? Pupils' attributions of success and failure are very important influences here. Some attribute success to 'luck' and failure to 'being thick'; others attribute success to 'ability' and failure to 'bad luck' or 'not trying'; while still others will explain their success or failure in terms of good or bad teaching, or whether or not they like the teacher, or think that the teacher likes them.[14] Such attributions will influence students' subjective estimates of the likelihood of success arising from different stances. If I think that my failure is due to lack of effort, I am crediting myself with the capability or the resources to do better. If I think it is due to lack of ability, then I have no control, and trying to understand will be a waste of time. And if I put it down to bad luck, then I might carry on in the same old way, waiting for my luck to change. Such examples show clearly that learners' implicit theories about what is going on are no mere abstractions but are crucial determinants of how they really respond and what they really learn.

What external resources are available to me?

Some considerations place the emphasis on how learners construe their situations rather than how they construe themselves (though, as you will have seen, there can be no clear separation). In assessing the external resources, a learner will be tacitly asking certain questions. Am I likely to have the time to go into this in the depth that I would like? If I am going to swot, am I going to get support at home for doing my homework, and be able to find a place to study where I cannot hear the television? Do I trust the teachers enough to be able to ask them when I do not understand (without feeling anxious or embarrassed)? Are my friends likely to provide me with moral as well as intellectual support? Negative answers to such questions will lead the learner towards a choice of classroom stance that neither seeks nor hopes for success in understanding and achievement.

What kind of learning is the subject going to require?

A learner has to make an informed guess about the kinds of learning that are going to be required by a particular subject and encouraged by the classroom ethos created and teaching style used by a particular teacher. How much remembering is going to be involved? Will I be able to express my own opinions and ideas? How much practical work will be required (I am hopeless with my hands)? These sorts of consideration, involved in the attempt to weigh up the intrinsic demands of certain subjects against the personal resources that students think they have ('what they are good at'), are particularly evident at the time in the third year when fourth-year options are being considered. At that time other considerations are also involved: a trip to the 'vocational guidance' person to see if there is any way of becoming a nurse without having to do chemistry; and appeals to friends' older brothers and sisters to find out 'what Mrs Dimmock's really like'. But I am suggesting that these kinds of question are being tacitly asked, and existing answers are being re-examined and modified, throughout a young person's school career.

What costs and risks are involved in different choices?

Costs are those negative consequences that I predict will follow from various courses of action. Risks are negative consequences that I fear might result. There is a particular set of costs and risks that I wish to highlight here that is associated with the process of learning. Learning in general is a risky business because it means moving out from the safety of the known into the unknown and the uncontrolled. What are these risks? The first is a loss of competence. Learners are probably going to make mistakes and errors of judgement as they explore ways of reading and dealing with novel situations. Second, there may be a loss of clarity. The learner feels confused and at sea, without a clear mental framework within which to understand what is going on. Third, there is often a loss of consistency, by which I mean that learners may find themselves acting, thinking or feeling in ways that are inconsistent with their image or picture of themselves. As one experiments with different stances, for example, one may find oneself responding in ways that feel alien or out of character. Fourth, there may well be a loss of composure. The learner feels intermittently anxious, frustrated, irritable or distressed. The involvement of emotion in learning, especially any learning that involves personal risks of the kinds described, seems inevitable.[15]

   Yet many learners, both younger and older, seem to have lost some of their ability to tolerate these experiences. To see why this is, we need to refer back to the topic we raised in Chapter 2: people's implicit theories. But now we are interested not in their detached views about learning, but rather in the personal beliefs they hold that influence their capability as learners. Especially we need to uncover the assumptions that people have commonly made about two key issues: their own worth, and the nature of ability. We shall see that certain attitudes in these two areas actually undermine people's ability to tolerate learning. They make the risks of learning seem even higher than they are, so that people are led to adopt stances that are more defensive than they need to be. We shall examine each of these areas in turn.

PERSONAL WORTH

Buried in many people's personal belief systems are implicit theories of what it means to be a mature, worthwhile person, which set limits on the conditions under which we may have 'high self-esteem' – that is, feel good about ourselves. These beliefs frequently include the following:

1. Worthwhile people do not make mistakes. Worth is contingent on competence. Incompetence is unworthy and must be paid for with guilt, shame or a loss of self-esteem.
2. Worthwhile people always know what is going on. Worth is contingent on clarity. Confusion and feeling out of control are unworthy and should be paid for with a loss of self-esteem.
3. Worthwhile people live up to, and within, their images of themselves. Worth is contingent on consistency. Acting unpredictably, out of character or in defiance of one's precedents and principles is unworthy and must be paid for with a loss of self-esteem.
4. Worthwhile people do not feel anxious, apprehensive, fraught or fragile. Worth is contingent on feeling cool, calm and collected. Feeling nervous, overwhelmed or ill-tempered should be paid for with a loss of self-esteem.[16]

What this means is that a person subject to these unconscious programming instructions will feel undermined and threatened by experiences that are necessary concomitants of many forms of learning, especially those, common at school age, that involve the learner's personality and styles of relating. Instead of being a precarious and difficult transition from a limited competence to an expanded one, the whole process can also come to feel like an assault on one's belief in oneself. People feel threatened by learning, and the rational response to perceived threat, for people as for animals, is defence. Instead of dealing with the unknown by engaging with it and mastering it (choosing a learning strategy), the threatened person judges the situation too dangerous to explore, and opts instead for a strategy that is designed to preserve or maintain what they already know, or can do, or are.

If we were not equipped to preserve ourselves in the face of apparent danger, we would not be much good at survival. The ability to be effectively defensive is, as I said before, a vital one. The problem arises when we misjudge events, so that we engage with what is actually dangerous (an unexploded bomb on waste land, a sarcastic and sadistic teacher) or flee from what is actually safe (somebody you fancy, a gruff but kindly teacher). This is precisely what 'the four Cs' – the commitments to competence, consistency, clarity and cool – lead us to do. They make us overestimate the dangers of learning, so that the learning that we really want or need to do is made to seem too hazardous to pursue. When this happens the search for mastery is abandoned in favour of the now more pressing search for ways of bolstering self-esteem or escaping from the threatening situation.

ABILITY

The cost–benefit analysis is distorted and 'loaded', like a biased dice, when we put into it inaccurate estimates of the risks to personal worth, or of the ability we possess. We can only dare to do what we think we can. Or as Henry Ford said, 'Those who believe they can do something and those who believe they can't are both right'.[17] A belief in low ability becomes a self-fulfilling prophecy. But some recent research by Carol Dweck in America has shown that we are belittled not only by underestimating the level of ability we possess; the very way we conceive of ability itself also has a powerful effect on the stances we adopt towards learning.[18]

Dweck's research has investigated the proneness of different children to lapse into a kind of 'helpless' stance following the experience of failure or frustration. The components of this stance are familiar to everyone, I am sure: tending to give up; regressing to less effective strategies; feeling badly about yourself; comparing yourself negatively with others; getting upset or angry. By giving children of different ages a variety of questionnaires and interviews, she discovered that the helpless-prone tended to have acquired certain views about their ability. Many of these children had developed a self-image in which they saw themselves as confirmed 'failures', and it was this, rather than the objective truth about their capabilities as learners, that determined their helpless response. It appears that, once an idea like 'I am a failure' becomes embedded in a person's implicit theory about themselves, it acquires the status of a self-fulfilling prophecy.

But Dweck discovered another significant belief-system underlying the particular attitude towards the level of one's own ability, which concerned the way the children construed the idea of 'ability' itself. The helpless-prone children saw ability as a fixed 'thing' which determined absolutely how 'bright' or 'thick' one was, and which could not be increased. In this world-view, school is about demonstrating successfully, to your own and other people's satisfaction, that you 'have' a certain level of ability. Failure and frustration demonstrate the reverse. The children who were challenged by difficulty rather than threatened by it (whom Dweck calls 'mastery-oriented') have the contrary belief about ability: they see it as a fluid quality that can be increased. It is possible to get 'smarter'. Failure for them is an opportunity to do just that: to 'sharpen their wits'. Thus the theories that teachers may hold about ability, which we discussed in Chapter 3, can have serious repercussions for the way pupils learn if those beliefs are transmitted, however subtly, in the classroom.

ENHANCING SELF-ESTEEM

There is much talk in education today about the importance of establishing or enhancing 'good self-esteem'. The analysis I have given here shows that this can mean two quite different things. One view is to leave the implicit theories where they are and to try to ensure that children are shielded from experiences which conflict with them. If pupils are upset by failure, give them a special diet of constant success, for instance. The trouble with this approach, as Dweck has shown, is that it is like making sure that someone who is agoraphobic has a nice house and plenty of food in the freezer. Constant success does nothing for your ability to cope with the inevitable, eventual, failure. In fact it may well make you even less able to keep your cool. A good measure of well-intentioned niceness does not cure the problem; at best it just postpones it, and at worst it exacerbates it.

The more radical way to enhance self-esteem is to tackle the underlying beliefs which are rendering esteem vulnerable in the first place, by helping – training, if necessary – pupils to interpret their experience differently. For example, in one of her early studies[19] Carol Dweck first identified two groups of children aged from 8 to 13 years old on the basis of teachers' and educational psychologists' reports. One group, the 'helpless-prone' (HP), were likely to give up and feel badly when they encountered failure. The other, the 'mastery-oriented' (MO), used more effort and even developed more sophisticated learning strategies when they failed. The two groups did not differ in their 'ability' as judged by their teachers. By giving them questionnaires, she found that the HP group were significantly more likely to believe that failure was due to a lack of ability, while the MO group attributed failure to not expending enough effort. She then gave both groups a series of maths problems to do over a period of twenty-five days, some of which they would fail. After a failure, half the HP group were told 'that means you should have tried harder'. Sure enough, after this training, this group of helpless-prone pupils had become much more like the mastery-oriented pupils. They gave up less easily, and attributed their failures more to a lack of effort. The trainer's comments had apparently helped them to change their implicit theory, so that failure had come to be seen as (1) less of an attack on their self-worth, and (2) something they could actually do something about (by 'trying'). Although this study was carried out on only a small number of children (twenty-two in all) it has since been repeated with the same results.

OTHER RISKS

As well as personal risks and costs, there may be intellectual and social ones. For example, some teachers see their main job as being to unearth pupils' social and working knowledge about a topic – 'motion' or 'peace', say – and to encourage them to replace this way of thinking, talking and acting with a more 'soundly based' theory or vocabulary. But this is a considerable demand in terms of learning, for it requires students to expose their own informal implicit theories, to juxtapose them with an initially alien and abstract view, and to abandon the former for the latter.[20] They have to construct a learning stance within which these different forms of knowledge can meet and talk to each other, and the intellectual investment required may be considerable.

In addition, students who opt to go along with this may find themselves increasingly out of sympathy with the habitual modes of thinking of their family and friends, and may begin to feel alienated from their home culture. Parents may become critical of their 'fancy language', or say 'We can't talk to Susan any more; she's getting too smart for her own good'. (The film *Educating Rita* shows such a reaction.) Considerable tensions may be experienced by children living in traditional 'working-class' cultures if they begin to adopt too much the values and habits of school.[21] Some pupils will quite sensibly take such costs into account when deciding on their stance towards school.

DIFFERENCES BETWEEN PUPILS

The notion that each learner is involved in an inner decision-making process about how to make the best of a social situation, one important component of which is the opportunity to learn what the teacher is offering, provides a natural starting point for thinking about some of the different ways in which adolescents respond to such a situation. Some youngsters, mainly but by no means exclusively from middle-class families, will be equipped by their backgrounds with repertoires of interests and learning strategies that match quite closely those embedded in the traditional school curriculum. Their social knowledge, their ways of talking and thinking, will accord more naturally with that of their teachers, and their intellectual efforts will receive support and encouragement from home. Other young people will have grown up with quite another kind of social culture, one in which forms of talk are different and intellectual, social and practical forms of knowledge are evaluated differently.

Thus, although the selection and creation of strategies and stances is a personal, individual process, the ingredients that go into it, in terms of opportunities, risks and resources, depend very heavily on social and cultural factors. Many young people find that they have much less elbow room in school than others. It is perfectly possible for someone to be a black swot or a female boffin, but in many pupil (and sometimes teacher) cultures the social costs are prohibitively high. Sexism and racism operate in school, as elsewhere, by creating webs of expectations and pressures that push white boys, but more importantly girls and people from ethnic minorities, in particular directions. It is not only that they are, in some ways, actually prevented from selecting from a more diverse, and more esteemed, set of options. Prejudice also works in an insidious fashion by setting up unnecessary internal constraints which serve to bias the outcomes of the cost–benefit analysis. It can permit choices but also load the psychological dice so that an unusual degree of self-confidence or social independence is required to take them. The most difficult form of cultural 'oppression' to overcome is when a person unwittingly adopts other people's false assumptions about her as her own.

Pupils' decision-making process may not always be as conscious and explicit as it is at the crucial times of selecting subject 'options', but it is at least potentially continuous, and an encounter with a teacher, or a surprising result on a test, can bring about a change of stance at any time. For example, children arriving in secondary school show a uniform, conformist 'honeymoon' stance for the first few weeks, but after that different, individualized repertoires of stances begin to emerge quite quickly.[22] Pupils also tend to shift their stances between different subjects. In order to maximize both achievement and peer acceptance/approval, for instance, it is quite common for an individual to adopt swot stance in high-status subjects like maths and English, while recouping public esteem by becoming socialite or joker in lower-status subjects like music or art.[23] Sometimes pupils have been observed shifting stances even within single lessons as they take up membership of different groups within the class.[24]

However, it is also true that pupils may make a once-and-for-all decision about a particular subject or teacher, or even about school as a whole. Some adolescents make up their minds quite firmly about how they are going to be in school, then stick to it, so that their stance becomes seen as a 'trait' and it functions as a self-fulfilling prophecy (I'm thick, so I don't try, so I don't succeed, so I'm thick). When a stance becomes habitual and self-sealing in this way, it is very difficult for an outsider (a teacher) to get the learner to re-evaluate decisions he has made (within the vicious circle, the more you try to convince me of my talents, the more obvious it is to me that you do not understand me at all, and that you are just another insincere, middle-class liberal trying to curry favour with me to stop me being 'difficult').

Let me give three little pen-pictures to reinforce the point that 'school' presents dramatically different problems to pupils, and that an equally diverse set of stances is to be expected. Sally, a 13-

year-old from Reading, is up at 5.30 a.m. several mornings a week rowing for the girls' novice eight, is secretary of the school council, plays flute in the chamber orchestra two lunchtimes a week, works hard in most subjects and is trying to decide whether she has a boyfriend or not. She is a classic 'good kid', adept at being naughty enough to win peer approval, and good enough to please the teachers. She has the self-confidence to share her creative efforts with the family at dinner-time, but goes into paroxysms of defence and rationalization when she thinks she has made a social gaffe (and 'behaved like a kid'). She does jazz ballet after school on Tuesdays and a music lesson on Thursdays, and is worrying why her periods have not started yet. (No wonder she spends all the rest of her waking time watching Bugs Bunny and *Neighbours*.)

If school stresses Sally by offering her too many chances to learn and grow, it stresses many other adolescents for entirely different reasons. Nasima is also 13, the fifth of seven children in an Asian family who live over their shop in West London. Her parents came to England from Bangladesh when she was 5. She is engaged to be married to the son of distant relatives who now live in India, a boy she will not meet for another four years at least. She is good at schoolwork and wants to have a career of her own – she hopes to be a doctor. She is very pretty but is teased by the boys at school because her parents will not permit her to wear Western clothes. She is extremely shy and has found her own secret place at school where she can eat her lunch by herself. She has to get up early and be home straight after school to look after her two little brothers whom she adores. Finding somewhere quiet to do her homework is a continual problem. She usually feels tired and frequently gets headaches, which she has never told her parents. She reads a lot of romantic fiction, but feels guilty about doing so: her father would be furious if he ever found out.

Then there is Ralph. He is an only child living with his mother. He has never seen his father. Ralph is fat and scruffy and has a moderate hearing loss. He sits at the front of the class staring at the teacher, trying to lip-read. He has a hearing aid but mostly refuses to wear it. He is very well-meaning and always has his hand up, but is hopeless at all his schoolwork except art. He constantly tries to make friends with the other kids and seems undaunted by their equally persistent efforts to ignore him. His mother, a university lecturer in education, fusses about his deafness and unwittingly encourages him to blame his handicap for his lack of maturity. She enjoys it when he is ill and they both have to stay home for the day.

Each of the three children finds school a totally different experience: each has to develop strategies for responding to the unique set of pressures, priorities and constraints that he or she experiences. While there are some generalizations that can be made on the basis of a pupil's race, class or gender, it is the way each person deals with the complex, dynamic and idiosyncratic nature of the predicament that will determine his or her stance towards lessons, and the learning that accrues. The existence of oppression and prejudice is anathema, and school, above all institutions in society, has a duty to reduce them in whatever ways possible: by example, by exhortation, by policy and by education itself. But the complementary concern, the assertion of which does nothing to deny the legitimacy and the need for social and political action, is with the freeing of individuals' minds from the 'invisible worm', as William Blake put it, of those false self-attributions that create fear, limit intelligence and distort perception. It is with this that the final chapter is concerned.

SUMMARY AND READING

Where previous chapters have concentrated on the processes of learning itself, this one has shown how learning can, and must, be seen within the whole context of a person's life. The device that was used for doing this, in as natural a way as possible, was to look at the multiple considerations that determine the incessant unconscious choices that people make about when, where, why and how to learn – or not learn. We illustrated this tacit decision-making process by showing that young people create and select between stances towards school that constitute packages of measures, of which learning strategies are a part, for dealing with the whole predicament of being in school. Some rather stereotyped stances were described to give the flavour of the analysis, whilst acknowledging that individuals must make personal choices in the light of their own estimations of the important considerations. As well as being concerned with learning, each stance may also provide methods for self-defence in the face of real or perceived threats of various sorts: to self-image and other personal beliefs, and to public standing. Some of these defensive strategies were described, and briefly exemplified in the school lives of both pupils and teachers. Belief in 'ability' as an immutable index of personal worth seemed to be a particular problem faced by many pupils.

In so far as this chapter has embedded learning back into the real life of schools, it is indebted to the ethnographic work of several, mostly British, sociologists. See for a good introduction the two sets of articles edited by M. Hammersley and P. Woods, *The Process of Schooling* and *Life in School: The Sociology of Pupil Culture*. However, this work nearly always ignores the specific learning opportunities that are available, for example in different subjects, and in that respect the present approach differs. I have also drawn again on the social psychological work of the 'attribution theorists' mentioned in Chapter 2. Carol Dweck's work is at the forefront of a trend in educational research, to which this chapter belongs, which is trying to find ways in which social, emotional and motivational influences can be naturally integrated with the cognitive approach to learning. A good general introduction to defensive strategies is provided by D. Hamachek's *Encounters with the Self*.[25]

NOTES

(1) Oscar Wilde, *The Importance of Being Earnest*. In Maine, G. F. (ed.) (1948) *The Works of Oscar Wilde*. London: Collins.

(2) Ethnographic research has been much in vogue amongst British sociologists of education in the last few years. It involves recording what actually goes on in schools, and what the real participants actually say and think about their situation, and it is therefore a valuable antidote to the traditional educational literature which concerns itself with idealized models and rhetoric about what *ought* to be happening.

(3) 'Conformist' by Woods, P. (1984) Negotiating the demands of schoolwork. In Hammersley, M. and Woods, P. (eds), *Life in School: The Sociology of Pupil Culture*. Milton Keynes: Open University Press. 'Compliant' by Turner, G. (1983) *The Social World of the Comprehensive*. Beckenham, Kent: Croom Helm.

(4) McLaren, P. (1986) *Schooling as a Ritual Performance*. London: Routledge & Kegan Paul.

(5) Fuller, M. (1984) Black girls in a London comprehensive school. In

Hammersley and Woods, *Life in School*, op. cit.

(6)   Beynon, J. (1985) *Initial Encounters in the Secondary School*. Lewes: Falmer.

(7)   Ibid.

(8)   Ibid.

(9)   Some of the most common pupil defences are mentioned by Hargreaves, D. (1982) *The Challenge for the Comprehensive School*. London: Routledge & Kegan Paul; and by Ernst, K. (1972) *Games Students Play*. Millbrae, CA: Celestial Arts. The defences used by staff are more fully described in Claxton, G. L. (1989) *Being a Teacher: A Positive Approach to Change and Stress*. London: Cassell.

(10)   See Mildiner, L. and House, B. (1974) *The Gates*. London: Centerprise, for an autobiographical account of two such phobics.

(11)   See Dunham, J. (1984) *Stress in Teaching*. Beckenham, Kent: Croom Helm; and Claxton, *Being a Teacher*, op. cit.

(12)   For the full clinical picture, see Rowe, D. (1983) *Depression: The Way out of Your Prison*. London: Routledge & Kegan Paul.

(13)   Ernst, *Games Students Play*, op. cit.

(14)   Burns, R. B. (1982) *Self Concept Development and Education*. London: Holt Education.

(15)   Levitt, E. E. (1980) *The Psychology of Anxiety*, 2nd edn. Hillsdale, NJ: Erlbaum.

(16)   For further discussion and justification of these beliefs, see Claxton, G. L. (1984) *Live and Learn: An Introduction to the Psychology of Growth and Change in Everyday Life*. London: Harper & Row, chapter 6; reissued (1988) Milton Keynes: Open University Press; and Claxton, *Being a Teacher*, op. cit., chapter 3.

(17)   Quoted by Walsh, R. (1984) *Staying Alive: The Psychology of Human Survival*. Boulder, CO: Shambhala.

(18)   Dweck, C. S. (1986) Motivational processes affecting learning. *American Psychologist*, **41**, 1040–8. Dweck, C. S. and Leggett, E. L. (1988) A social-cognitive approach to motivation and personality. *Psychological Review*, **95**, 256–73.

(19)   Dweck, C. S. (1987) The role of expectations and attributions in the alleviation of learned helplessness. *Journal of Personality and Social Psychology*, **31**, 674–85.

(20)   This has been explored in the area of science learning by Hewson, P. W. (1981) A conceptual change approach to learning science. *European Journal of Science Education*, **3**, 383–96.

(21)   Jackson, B. and Marsden, D. (1986) *Education and the Working Class*. London: Ark.

(22)   Ball, S. J. (1980) Initial encounters in the classroom and the process of establishment. In Woods, P. (ed.), *Pupil Strategies*. Beckenham, Kent: Croom Helm.

(23)   Measor, L. (1984) Pupil perceptions of subject status. In Goodson, I. F. and Ball, S. J. (eds), *Defining the Curriculum*. Lewes: Falmer.

(24) Furlong, V. J. (1976) Interaction sets in the classroom. I. Hammersley, M. and Woods, P. (eds), *The Process of Schooling.* London: Routledge & Kegan Paul.

(25) Hammersley and Woods, *The Process of Schooling*, op. cit., and *Life in School*, op. cit. Hamachek, D. (1987) *Encounters with the Self*, 3rd edn. New York: Holt, Rinehart & Winston.

8

Teaching for Learning

If you want to make sense, I've learned, you should never use the word should or ought until after you've used the word if.

John Barth[1]

In this final chapter I am going to examine the implications of this psychology for teaching and for schooling. But let me first recap on what the *kinds* of implication might be. Psychology can only give us ideas about what is going on in people's minds in given circumstances, and suggestions as to what else might go on if the circumstances were different. It is then a matter of value judgement, of one's educational philosophy, as to which alternative is preferred.

So first we can look for implications that arise from understanding better the conditions that facilitate or impede learning of different kinds. Teachers doing more or less orthodox jobs, in orthodox schools, with orthodox aims, might be enabled to work more efficiently. Specifically, we might be able to see more clearly which of the existing aims are compatible, in the sense that they can be approached via the same sets of conditions, and which may require different conditions for their achievement. If aims of education are incompatible in this sense, this does not mean that we have to abandon some of them entirely; rather we have to think in terms of tackling them at different ages, perhaps, or even interdigitating them over the same period. Thus there may be implications for policy as well as for the classroom practice of individual teachers.

It may be that psychological clarification of what is possible has repercussions also for our sense of what is desirable if, for example, options that previously had not been discerned, or had been discerned only vaguely, or which had seemed incapable of implementation, are revealed as conceivable and practicable. This still does not make them desirable, but it expands the debate about what *is* desirable.

My main conclusions will be that schools at present are not reliably equipping young people to be good learners; that this is because the aim of creating good learning is too vaguely specified at present, and is incompatible with other, more clearly held aims; but that such an aim can now be made both precise and achievable – it can be added to our list of practicable candidates for educational goals. I do not claim that fostering good learning is a new idea, only that it has hitherto been a relatively weak member of a confused portfolio of educational priorities, and that any rhetorical commitment to it has been honoured more in the breach than in the observance.

At this point, with a flourish, I replace my psychologist's hard hat with an ideologue's cap, and proclaim that if we *can* do it we *should* do it, at least at some ages: that there is no more vital need for young people today than that they should be able to learn well, and that this aim should not be allowed to be subverted by any other consideration.

THE PSYCHOLOGY SUMMARIZED

The first thing we need to do is to summarize the main points of the position at which we have arrived.

1. All learners, pupils and teachers, are in the business of making sense of the world around them. They can do this only by interpreting it in terms of what they already know. However unambiguous a fact or lesson or a concept may seem, it can be understood only in terms of a personal interpretation by the learner. This does *not* mean that we should not teach groups of learners together, or that we are debarred from trying to influence them to think and act in certain ways.

2. Knowledge is organized into mental packages ('minitheories') that are developed to provide clear interpretation and smooth

expertise in familiar domains of experience. These modules can and do become more generalized, and more interlinked, but this is a slow, and always incomplete, evolutionary process. Learning *when to use* what we know is as important a form of learning as increasing *what* we know.

3. Minitheories are 'indexed' not only according to the specific kinds of content to which they apply, but also in terms of the complete social, emotional and physical context in which they have been developed. The more unvarying this context is, the less opportunity there is to learn to 'disembed' the skills that have been developed within it. Relevance must always be discovered: its perception can never be taken for granted.

4. The minitheory we happen to be 'running' represents our assumption about what *kind* of situation we find ourselves in. The currently active minitheory determines what knowledge and skill are available to us, and how we interpret the significance of what is happening. Knowledge and skill that is not contained on the active 'file' is functionally unavailable to us. We will act as if we did not have it.

5. There is a *natural learning ability*, under the influence of which a person's mental landscape of minitheories grows and develops. This ability enables us to extend existing minitheories to cover new events, and to modify their contents (TALEs) and their indexing (HEADs) in the light of experience.

6. A crucial thread within human development is the discovery of skills for dealing with certain kinds of 'problem' – events that do not succumb easily to the application of existing content-specific processes. At first, like all skills, these 'learning strategies' develop within a particular domain; but they may become relatively disembedded and therefore more widely available.

7. The development of learning strategies is an organic, not a mechanistic, process. Conditions may certainly be more or less congenial to their growth, and strategies can be identified and described, but this does not lead to the conclusion that they are independent abilities that can be sequenced and trained; assembled inside a learner's head as if they were 'cogs' out of which a smoothly running clockwork cognition could be constructed.

8. People's learning varies not just in amount, or in accuracy, but in kind, depending on the knowledge that is available to them

at the time, the knowledge 'format' of the active file, the attentional set that the file creates, and the particular learning strategies that the file contains or to which it gives access. Through this process the conditions that teachers wittingly or unwittingly create influence how people approach a learning task and the kinds of mental product that accrue.

9. There are no content-free cognitive processes. What we usually call 'ability' or 'intelligence' is a particular set of learnable strategies which happen to be well suited for the kind of learning required for success in school. As with other minitheories, each learning strategy must have attached to it an accurate, intuitive sense of its scope and limitations. This sense arises, as it does with any art, through the exercise of responsibility to choose, and freedom to experiment, within a context that strikes an appropriate balance between being challenging and safe.

10. Unless people are profoundly depressed or disabled, whatever they are doing makes sense to them. The 'stance' they adopt represents their attempt to maximise their interests (including altruistic ones) and minimize the threats (including imagined ones) within the situation as they perceive it.

11. Pupils' stances in schools are 'solutions' to the problem of how best to *be*, in a predicament that includes motivational, emotional, personal, social and cultural ingredients, as well as cognitive ones. A teacher may play a leading or an insignificant role in this predicament.

12. How, and how much, to learn of the official subject matter of school is a question that is answered by pupils in terms of the predicament as a whole. To get the complex 'equation' to balance may require pupils to try their best, or it may lead them to underachieve.

13. It is as important, and as intelligent, for pupils and teachers to defend themselves against perceived threat as it is for them to explore perceived opportunities and challenges. A repertoire of defensive strategies is as useful to survival as a good 'tool-kit' of learning strategies. If a pupil construes the classroom situation as potentially threatening to self-respect or group acceptance, then defence may predominate over learning in her adopted stance.

14. Stances are selected and created on the basis of an intuitive 'cost–benefit analysis' which weighs up perceived opportunities, priorities, resources, costs and risks. If any of these ingredients are

*mis*perceived, then the outcome of this rational, largely tacit, decision-making process will be a sub-optimal or even self-defeating stance. It may, for example be, reckless (if risks are underestimated), over-cautious (if they are exaggerated), impractical (if opportunities are seen where there are none), grandiose (if personal resources are overestimated), defeatist (if self-image prohibits sensible solutions) and so on.

15. When competence, mental clarity and a sense of control and of emotional comfort are taken as valid indices of personal worth, self-esteem becomes contingent on the avoidance (or at least the covering-up) of mistakes, confusion, anxiety or feeling at sea. Any learning experience that contains these risks is therefore construed as a potential threat, and is likely to be met with a defensive, rather than an exploratory, stance.

16. When self-image represents 'ability' as a fixed, pervasive, monolithic entity, this implicit view becomes a self-fulfilling prophecy, biasing pupils towards a stance of *proving* their competence, rather than *improving* it.

17. Pupils' decision-making processes incorporate estimates of *perceived* ability and do not therefore reflect *actual* ability (as defined in paragraph 9 above) unless the internal self-assessment is accurate – something which teachers cannot confidently know. Nothing can be inferred, therefore, from pupils' achievement or their demeanour about their 'ability level' or their 'personality'.

18. External conditions which influence stance-selection include the classroom culture; peer beliefs, pressures and expectations; parental expectations; teacher style and attitudes; and personal and institutional attitudes to gender, class, ethnicity, 'ability', disability, sexuality, 'childhood', 'adolescence' and so on.

19. Many pupils achieve badly in school because their personal and social predicament seems to require the sacrifice of growth for self-preservation. This is a rational solution to an 'equation' that contains limited opportunities, an inaccurate self-image, and conditioned fears of various sorts. Seen from their side, it may well be perfectly intelligent to act 'stupid'.

20. Much of teachers' influence on the development of young people's learning is achieved through their informal, unguarded language and the implicit theories that they hold, whether knowingly or not. If teachers are not themselves good learners, they arrest both their own development and that of their pupils,

via the implicit messages which they broadcast about what to value and what to fear.

GOOD LEARNERS

This psychology says that people's power as learners is affected by their experience, and it points to conditions that may either undermine or develop that power. Before looking at the options that teachers have in this matter, let us pull together the ideas, implicit in what we have discussed before, about what it means to be a 'good learner'. It means having 'learning positive' attitudes: being oriented towards seeing and seizing learning opportunities when they are congruent with the learner's own priorities and interests. Closely linked with this is the need for emotional resilience: the ability to tolerate making some mistakes, feeling in a mental fog, not having a firm grasp on what is going on, and being somewhat anxious or even frustrated. Good learners must not 'run for cover' in the face of such experiences. They need to view learning in general more as a challenge than as a threat. However, good learning also requires some healthy caution: not all unusual events are either necessary or safe to investigate, and a measure of judicious circumspection is also an asset. Generally, good learners need a realistic sense of their own resources – both psychological and in terms of the material or social support on which they could reasonably expect to be able to call if necessary.

These attitudes and qualities set the stage. They create the personal context within which good learning is possible. What is needed next are the learning strategies themselves. Good learners need *inspection* strategies for collecting good information; for getting the world – social, material or intellectual – to reveal itself. They need *ingenuity*: ways of generating good guesses about how to respond to a strange occurrence; reasoning, fantasizing, asking questions, looking things up, watching how other people do it, and the rest. Especially they need to have developed a good sense of the appropriateness of different techniques: when to rush in with a half-baked attempt; when to sit back and chew it over. They need to be capable of confident, convivial *interactions* with other people in seeking advice and in collaborating on joint projects. And finally they need *insight*: the capacity for clear awareness, and self-awareness, to be able to monitor what is happening, evaluate how the strategy is working, assess when to persist and when to adjust and reappraise priorities in the light of developing experience.

HOW DO YOU TEACH FOR GOOD LEARNING?

The successful teacher in traditional terms, especially at secondary level, wants pupils to understand and to master, and thereby to become more knowledgeable and skilful. If the best way to do that is to tell them and train them, then that is what to do. Pick out the key points and underline them. Explain difficult concepts clearly. Provide carefully planned and unambiguous experiments, exercises and experiences. Always give clear and unambiguous instructions. Provide examples of good practice, and explain *why* they are good. Point out the vital features that should distinguish one topic or type of problem from another. Encourage and reward success. Correct mistakes quickly and consistently. Try to anticipate pupils' difficulties or misconceptions and find ways round them. All these methods typify the 'good teacher'. Teaching like this maximizes the chances that pupils will be able to perform smoothly and successfully in situations – like most exams – that ask them to apply familiar operations to familiar content.

To make the contrast unnaturally strong, compare this picture with one of people whose top priority is to help pupils become good learners – let us call them *mentors*, for want of a better word. They work differently, because they see that the technique of the good *teacher* either fails to make much of an impression on pupils – those of 'low ability' – or makes them simultaneously successful with the familiar *and* vulnerable to the unfamiliar. They see that 'good pupils' are often thrown by failure; inclined to give up or to flounder in the face of novelty until they have been *told* how to tackle it; and resistant to innovation, made conservative in their attitude to learning by the acquired need to keep on succeeding, regardless of real intellectual growth. Good pupils often perform well and look good but at the expense of precisely those qualities that distinguish good learners: resourcefulness, persistence and creativity. And it is just this kind of quality that mentors care about. Their main concern is to equip their pupils with the ability to be intelligent in the face of change.

Organization

The form of organization that mentors would adopt gives a measure of responsibility and choice to learners, but it is by no means *laissez-faire*. The point is to arrange learning experiences in such a way that they provoke learners into extending their learning power, whilst also giving time for the limitations of their learning strategies to be intuitively grasped by the learners, so that they acquire a feel for their range of applicability. This means giving learners the chance to discover for themselves, through their own guided exploration, what each of their strategies is good for, and what it is not good for. While the appropriate way of thinking and learning is prescribed for them, they have no opportunity to assess for themselves when to struggle for understanding and when to commit to memory; when to reason logically and when to reflect intuitively; when to develop tacit expertise and when it helps to be able to describe what you are doing. Not having an intuitive sense of the scope and the limitations of rational analysis, for example, people are at risk of abandoning rationality entirely when they encounter, as they surely will, occasions when it does not provide any answers – leaving themselves, perhaps, with only the most rudimentary and undeveloped tools with which to learn. By overemphasizing rational thought, school paradoxically sets at least some of its clients up to be prey to impulsiveness.

Learners' responsibility, which may be circumscribed but which must be quite real, must go hand in hand with the variety that is essential if the transfer problem is to be overcome. If a learning strategy is acquired through working on only one kind of problem in only one kind of context with only one kind of subject matter, and worse, if all this is predetermined by a teacher, then we should not be surprised if it remains tied to those conditions – as the evidence suggests that it will.

Reflectivity

To be a mentor means encouraging pupils to develop and strengthen the higher-order learning strategies of monitoring and self-awareness, so that they develop their own sense of when and how to be persistent and when to adjust. Good learners must be able to keep track of how their learning is going and if necessary to take stock and experiment with new kinds of approach. (The popular books on 'lateral thinking' by Edward de Bono give plenty of examples of how we tend to be too dogged and unadventurous in our approach to problems, and of the value of being able to switch out of logical learning strategies into alternative modes that are less rational but more creative.[2]) Mentors will not correct 'mistakes' much, for this deprives pupils of opportunities to spot and analyse their own. They will not keep interfering: even when they see pupils reinventing the wheel (wrongly) they will be inclined to hold back – because they remember that the important thing is the inventing, not the rolling.

Learning strategies, especially the powers of self-monitoring and self-awareness (like all abilities), develop only through use. So up to a point mentors will not seek to make learning endlessly smooth and successful: they must be prepared to let learners run into difficulties, in order to be able to develop the metacognitive abilities that they need to sort themselves out. They might deliberately leave a manageable amount of ambiguity in their instructions, encouraging pupils to figure them out for themselves, and thus developing the skill of finding their way out of the wood – without panicking. Instead of pointing out the key points, they are more likely to ask pupils to dig them out themselves, either alone or in discussion with each other. Wherever possible, they will introduce some genuine, even if only small, choices for pupils to make about what they do, how they do it, how they sequence and prioritize various tasks, and so on.

Production

Mentors will not insist that everything has to be completed. The 'product' is only an incidental outcome of the main business of learning to learn – though one that is necessary from time to time to create the confidence to keep trying and the satisfaction of a tangible result. There is nothing intrinsically admirable about always completing what you have started. (Yet many undergraduates insist on struggling on to the bitter end with books that are palpably boring, incomprehensible or irrelevant.) But mentors will also let pupils live with the consequences of giving up on tasks that they, the pupils, really do want to complete. Part of being a good learner is constantly monitoring whether you are getting anywhere, and whether it is still 'worth it'. Giving up because you believe that having to try shows that you are not very clever[3] is dysfunctional. Giving up because you genuinely have better things to do – that is intelligent.

Nor will mentors insist that answers must come quickly – for they recognize the importance of fostering the learning strategies that are less conscious and less fast-moving than those of rational thought. They know (because they probably do it themselves) that loafing about, doodling, gazing out of the window and chatting are not simple signs of 'lack of motivation' but are necessary breaks from more effortful, deliberate forms of learning, and are often the outward face of learning strategies that are valuable in their own right. Creativity arises from less focused, less purposeful modes of cognition that are contemplative and imaginative.

Sociability

Mentors will encourage pupils to be sociable in their learning, knowing that, for younger ones at least, sociability is more important than individual achievement, and is the womb within which more general cognitive skills need first to be grown. They also remember that there is much to be learnt, at both social and cognitive levels, from being a private in someone else's learning production, as well as a general in your own. They will encourage pupils to explain things to each other, knowing that the attempt to communicate what you know is a valuable learning exercise in its own right.

But as well as encouraging learners to be sociable, mentors will also permit them to be rather more private than is common in schools. For example, they will draw out flexibility of language, of the use of different voices, by encouraging learners to keep for-their-eyes-only jottings, diaries and half-baked reflections, and distinguishing clearly between the idiosyncratic, even cryptic, form that these will probably take and different requirements that pertain to different kinds of 'finished product'. Deliberately 'crossing' contrasting contents and forms, such as writing up an experiment in French, or setting an equation to music, would be useful as well as entertaining.

Nudging

Having achieved the right answer one way, mentors might ask
learners to see in how many other ways they can do it. They may
use fantasy and imagination to get learners to project what they
are discovering into real-life situations in which it will be useful –
and if possible will create real simulations and experiences of the
use of this learning in practice. They might invite them to gain
greater control over their learning strategies by deliberately
creating 'wrong' answers (for example, mistranslations of French
words, impossible climatic conditions, fallacious inferences from a
literary passage) and challenging their friends to figure out how
they reached them. Thus they stimulate learners to be interested in
and creative about their 'failures'.

   They might provide instances of good *and bad* practice, and ask
learners to sort them out for themselves, analysing the difference
along the way. They might ask learners to reflect, before tackling a
new problem, on which, if any, of those they have already mastered
it is like. They will often ask learners what they think about a topic
before they start to enquire into it, thus fostering the habit of being
active and questioning.

Responding

This way of 'teaching' leaves mentors with considerable
responsibility for selecting and sequencing activities. But as I have
stressed, we must avoid at all costs falling into the trap of believing
that learning strategies should be deliberately 'trained'. Such a
calculated, premeditated approach easily squeezes out the vital
element of freedom in the learners' explorations.[4] Yet I have also
stressed the importance of suiting the kind of experience, the
pacing of events and the amount of choice, to the learners' own
level of competence. How is this to be achieved? By listening.
Mentors demonstrate by their attentive attitude a genuine interest
in learners' interpretations, confusions and 'mistakes', because
only by trying to understand why an idea seems sensible to its
author can a mentor hope to provide the right sort of nudge. You
cannot put down a useful stepping stone for someone to find if you
do not have a clue where they are.

Thus the 'right' experience for a learner to be tackling is discovered by a process of seeing how the original is being received and making sensible suggestions as to how the activity could be modified. Learners end up with an appropriately challenging thing to do, and they are also learning, through the process of interaction and negotiation with the mentor, the rudiments of reflection about their own process. In discussion they begin to identify their own interests, abilities and areas of frustration.

It is *only* by being responsive to the learners' signals that the mentor can ensure that the evolution of learning continues in an integrated fashion and is not ruptured. When teachers are prevented from being responsive, learning stops being developmental and becomes laminar: levels of understanding become overlaid on each other rather than supplanting each other. A useful mentorial rule is not to allow yourself to offer any advice or information until you have first been able to rephrase a learner's current understanding and state of mind *to the learner's satisfaction*.

Climate setting

An important part of the mentors' role is to create a climate within which young people *feel* free to learn, and this means removing, as far as possible, the unnecessary risks to self-esteem with which learning is often surrounded, while at the same permitting without dramatizing them the inevitable feelings of frustration, disappointment and apprehension with which learning, in however safe a context, is always attended. Their job is to create an environment where tolerance for the frailties that learning requires is protected – where learners can be more interested in stretching themselves than in saving face.

But they need too to have a warm but matter-of-fact attitude to emotion when it inevitably appears. By their responses they must signal that feelings are not problems, and should show learners how to deal with them in the most skilful manner. This is one reason why 'time out' is so useful. When a learner has flipped into a negative mood, and is feeling 'helpless-prone' rather than 'mastery-oriented', to use Dweck's terms, the best thing to do is often something completely different. Have a chat or a cup of coffee. Read a novel for a while. See if anyone wants some help with *their* project. Have a snooze or stare out of the window. What is often less helpful is to work on the learning block, or the emotion, directly. When she is back on good form, the learner will probably be quite able to resolve the difficulty for herself, and will feel all the better for having done so. She will be more likely to trust herself to manage next time. By the same token, mentors will not reward or praise every effort, for doing so renders learners intolerant of frustration and dependent on an outsider for encouragement and feedback.

Modelling

Mentors, being sensitive to the conventional mixed messages of 'Don't do as I do; do as I say', will be interested in modelling, to the best of their ability, the skills and attitudes of good learning. They will have, if there is time, a public learning project of their own in the classroom, which learners are invited to contribute to and comment on. They will be good examples of people who can tolerate their own confusion (or even frustration), thus giving learners the opportunity to see and hear the real, dirty, time-consuming, reflective process of learning. They will be able to laugh at themselves when they make silly mistakes. They will be open to help, and willing to ask for it. And they will also model generosity towards and pleasure in other people's achievements.

Thinking aloud

Generally, mentors will be interested in the *process* of learning, and will take puzzlement as something to be worked on and talked about collaboratively. One of the things at which they need to be skilled is thinking out loud, especially when difficulties are encountered or tactical decisions have to be made. By externalizing their own thought processes, perhaps by thinking through the choice between different ways of tackling their own project, they will be demonstrating the learning strategies available, the decision-making processes and the ability to take time to fumble with uncertainties, all at the same time. Such modelling will have a much more significant impact on learners' developing abilities than any amount of direct instruction or exhortation.

Introspection

To be able to be such a model, mentors need to be interested in their own processes and reactions: one of their professional responsibilities (the seeds of which should be sown during their training) is to develop *self*-awareness about learning. By becoming more sensitive to their own feelings and reactions, they will develop greater tolerance and understanding for those of others, and will therefore be more likely to respond in a helpful, rather than in an unsubtle or even punitive, way. By becoming more aware of their own processes, they will be able to think out loud all the better. They will also become more conscious of the variety of attitudes that they had previously been inadvertently displaying as they interact in a host of ways with the learners.

Social and psychological attitudes

Mentors have to be generally sensitive to the character attributions they make in their written comments and their casual conversations with learners and with colleagues. They will slowly learn to resist the insidious temptation to talk about learners' achievement as if it were an index of 'ability', or to set learners' classroom demeanour in concrete by treating it as direct reflection of personality traits. They will not make it an issue when learners 'act out of character', knowing that experimenting with one's self-definition is one of the most important learning processes of all.

One of their own learning projects should be the effort to be increasingly aware of the subtle ways in which cultural, sexual and other stereotypes provide illicit assumptions which channel their interactions with learners in ways that are limiting or diminishing. Both in their individual dealings with young people and through the corporate decision-making that determines policy and ethos, mentors have to ensure that they are not transmitting and affirming cultural stereotypes of class, race, gender and physical endowment. Adolescents' ability to grow and develop is hampered by expectations that derive from collective mythology and that therefore impose socially enforced limits on what they are allowed or encouraged to become. These constrictions on development become firmer and tighter if institutional messages that such prejudices are acceptable reinforce those that are already dissolved in at least some of the codes that guide adolescents' interactions with each other. As well as equipping young people with the tools to learn, part of school's responsibility must be to provide the conditions that will permit such learning.

Campaigning

I have deliberately created a strong contrast between 'teaching' and 'mentoring', knowing that most real teachers are a combination of the two. But it is useful to highlight the ingredients of a teacher's role that are conducive to good learning and those that are not; and also to draw attention to the extent to which some key elements of the mentor's role are made difficult, if not impossible, by the current structure of schooling. Many teachers are doing, or trying to do, many of the things that enhance good learning. The problem that they face, with a greater or lesser degree of conscious awareness, is that much of what they are *required* to do, as conventional schoolteachers, pulls them in conflicting directions. The structure of syllabuses, timetables and examinations demands a form of education that, whatever the rhetoric says, actually works against the goal of good learning.

   I do not wish to embark on yet another critique of this recently reinforced paraphernalia here. All I wish to point out is that, as teachers develop a clearer idea of what teaching-for-good-learning means, and how to do it, so their deep but presently ill-formed frustration with the current pressures and constraints will themselves come into sharper relief, and they will be able to have more focused debates, and to mount more powerful campaigns, because what they are seeking will be that much better argued and expressed. They will know what they are *for*, as well as what they are against, and that makes a much harder manifesto to ignore. Hopefully this book will help provide a rationale for those teachers who like the sound of 'teaching to learn', and some ammunition to use as they promote their own variations on the theme.

In this sense the book is a companion volume to my *Being a Teacher: A Positive Approach to Change and Stress*, published in 1989. As I said in Chapter 1, that book focused on the techniques that teachers could use to keep as much of a sense of control over their professional destinies as possible – a sense that is vital, I suggested, precisely at a time when their elbow room seems to be being reduced. It argued that it is important to have something, albeit small, to care about and to promote, but it had relatively little to say about what such a cause might be. The present book is designed to identify the cause that *I* am trying to promote, to develop its rationale, and to see (as the Americans say) whether anybody salutes if I run it up the flagpole. Finally, it is time to come clean: to take off the dispassionate, intellectual hat and get up on my soap-box.

SHOULD SCHOOLS BE CONCERNED WITH GOOD LEARNING?

School has traditionally presupposed people's ability to learn and has focused on trying to mobilize such ability as people have in the service of expanding their store of knowledge and skill. This approach now not only lacks psychological plausibility; it is no longer educationally defensible. It is not educationally defensible for a host of reasons, of which I shall mention just three.

First, beyond a certain point formal knowledge and academic skills are not what young people need from school these days. Much of traditional school knowledge (including large parts of secondary school English, maths and science, the Education Reform Act notwithstanding) does not equip people to survive in a world of information explosion and information technology. The vast majority of physics graduates are no better able to fix their video recorders than the rest of us, and rhetoric about 'understanding a technological society' is a perfectly empty excuse for trotting out definitions of volts, amps and watts, or even giving third years plugs to wire up. In such a world, textbook knowledge is either remote or stale, and if young people want something fresher or more useful they can get it from TV, a piece of software or a public library.

Of course, there is some content – some information – that is good for youngsters to know, and not all of it is missing from the National Curriculum. But in a society where knowledge, values, jobs, technology and even styles of relationship are changing as fast as they are, it can be strongly argued that school's major responsibility must be to help young people become ready, willing and able to cope with change successfully: that is, to be powerful and effective learners.

The second point is this. Concern with the content emphasis has led, over the last few years, to a shift in the rationale of schooling from a preoccupation with *content* to a greater concern with *process* – with the acquisition of mental (and in some areas physical and social) skills. There is much talk now about teaching the skills of investigation, analysis, problem-solving and even, God help us, relationship, alongside traditional literacy and numeracy, and at least in some areas this is clearly a well-intentioned step. GCSE, attainment targets and programmes of study are awash with process language.

But the extent to which these much-vaunted skills transfer out of school appears to be remaining disappointingly low and unpredictable. Learners are frequently unable to take what is learnt in school and make it applicable to other contexts and purposes. As Nisbet and Shucksmith say in their book on learning strategies:

> Strategies [like these] are sometimes taught in school, but children do not learn to apply the strategies beyond specific applications in narrowly defined tasks. Effective learning requires more than this: skills and strategies have to be learnt in such a way that they can be transferred to fit new problems or situations not previously encountered. Being able to select the appropriate strategy, and adapt it where necessary, is an important part of this definition of good learning.[5]

If people do not understand the processes whereby transferability is discovered – if they are ignorant of the need for disembedding, and the attendant concerns with pacing and with the socioemotional nature of the old skin that usually needs to be sloughed – and merely suppose that transfer somehow *ought* to occur, then they are bound to be disappointed when it does not.

Third, if adolescents, at precisely the time in their lives when they are reassembling their personal, implicit theories of identity and worth, are exposed day-in, day-out to an institution whose agents and attitudes inculcate a sense of guilt or embarrassment about making mistakes, being confused, acting inconsistently and feeling 'weak', then their self-image is likely to incorporate these beliefs and to be built at the expense of their abilities as learners. Whether it knows it or not, a school that systematically both models and rewards a personal *investment* in competence, clarity, consistency and cool, is disempowering rather than empowering its students.

There is a wide concern that too many young people leave school disabled or even paralysed as learners, and preoccupied instead with saving face, covering up their frailities and detecting, avoiding or snuffing out even minimal threats to a sense of self-worth that is precariously balanced. For some of these young people, threatened by almost everything, yet forced by the injunction 'Thou shalt not look threatened' to appear to be threatened by nothing, all that may be left is a compulsive track of macho recklessness, manufactured confrontations and showing off. Others collapse into self-consciousness when asked to do anything that exceeds by the tiniest amount the narrow confines of their habitual, safe competence. It is hardly surprising that employers complain about 'the lack of initiative in some of today's young people'. Initiative is often just too risky.

If school is not equipping young people to be good learners in the world at large, then it is failing in what I would argue is its most important function. We have to throw away the old rationales which say that this is what we *hope* we are doing, and the discredited psychologies which claim that it somehow *ought* to happen, and acknowledge that it *is not* happening. The approach to learning that we have been developing provides a new perspective: one which says that helping young people is something we *can* do, but that it requires a different view of education. For example, as Howe attests:

> No educational objective is more important for students than learning how to learn, and how to function as an independent, autonomous learner. . ... A person who leaves school ill-equipped with the competencies required for learning independently throughout the remainder of a life is at a severe disadvantage.[6]

I believe that the form of schooling that we mostly still have remains largely inappropriate to the needs of young people growing up in an uncertain world. We do not help people to become good high-jumpers by building them a stepladder, or good swimmers by towing them up and down the pool at speed. We do not help them to become good learners by depriving them of responsibility and of the experience of making mistakes and living with the consequences. We do not help by labelling learners 'high' or 'low ability', or by giving them diets that consist of varying mixtures of personal failure and narrow success. The new psychology of learning shows that good learning is something that can be understood and enhanced; that education for good learning is a distinct possibility. This is good news to the many people in the education business who know that it is an absolute necessity.

NOTES

(1)   John Barth, *The Floating Opera* (1972). London: Bantam.
(2)   For example, de Bono, E. (1982) *De Bono's Thinking Course*. London: BBC Publications.
(3)   This is a feature of Carol Dweck's 'helpless-prone' pupils. See Dweck, C. S. (1986) Motivational processes affecting learning. *American Psychologist*, **41**, 1040–8.
(4)   Carr, M. and Claxton, G. L. (1989) The costs of calculation. *New Zealand Journal of Educational Studies*, **24**, 129–40.
(5)   Nisbet, J. and Shucksmith, J. (1986) *Learning Strategies*. London: Routledge & Kegan Paul.
(6)   Howe, M. J. A. (1984) *A Teacher's Guide to the Psychology of Learning*. Oxford: Blackwell.

Index